LONDON 1977–1987

BOOK ONE
The East End in Colour
1960–1980

BOOK TWO
The Isle of Dogs

BOOK THREE
Dog Show 1961–1978

BOOK FOUR
Paradise Street

BOOK FIVE
The East End in Colour
1980–1990

BOOK SIX
London Underground
1970–1980

BOOK SEVEN
Hackney Archive

BOOK EIGHT
Butlin's Holiday Camp
1982

BOOK NINE
London 1977–1987

LONDON 1977–1987

BERRIS CONOLLY

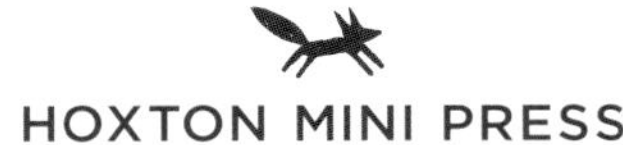

HOXTON MINI PRESS

INTRODUCTION

Anybody who's ever lived in or visited or even thought about London carries around with them their own mental version of the city, based on experience, history, rumour and myth. That's why we have Shakespeare's London, Dickens' London, Virginia Woolf's London, and even the Beatles' London. All these versions are 'true', even if they sometimes oppose or contradict each other. When it comes to photography, it seems there are as many versions of London as there are photographers, all creating work that sometimes supports and often undermines our existing idea of the city. Photographs of London date back almost to the very beginnings of photography itself – many claim the first to be a daguerreotype of Whitehall created by M. de St. Croix in 1839. After that, the deluge.

From the big names and usual suspects of the 20th century like Brandt, Beaton, Bailey and Bown (and that's just the Bs), all the way to Dougie Wallace and his uncompromising close-ups of shoppers outside Harrods, the list of photographers who have created significant work in the capital is very long indeed.

Berris Conolly has certainly paid his dues as a Londoner. He moved here aged 18 in 1966 and worked as an assistant to various photographers, including John Hedgecoe, who established a photography department at the Royal College of Art. After that he had various jobs in the commercial sector, then several years in a north London advertising studio, eventually giving it up in 1985, living on the dole, and pursuing his interest in independent documentary work.

Did Berris, or does any self-respecting photographer, ever take 'typical' or 'representative' photographs of London? No, because for a serious artist there's really no such thing as typical although inevitably an image that shows St Paul's Cathedral is going to be more recognisable to more people than one that shows Kingsland Road. Of course, good photographers want to avoid clichés. On the other hand, it would be possible to take photographs that make London look alien and unrecognisable, totally unlike itself, but what would be the point?

The mission is to create photographs of London that are both recognisable and unfamiliar, fresh but not gimmicky. This is where Berris Conolly succeeds. I have never seen London depicted quite the way it is in his photographs. They show parts of London that many people will never have seen, and even those who are familiar with, for instance the Hackney Marshes or Queensbridge Road, will find something here to surprise them.

The most recent of these pictures were taken over 30 years ago, which may seem a long time or comparatively recently depending on your point of view, but the London revealed doesn't strike me as wholly unfamiliar. Although the city shows its era in the cars, the street signs, the advertising billboards, the availability of parking, the way people are dressed, there's no yearning for the past and I detect very little nostalgia. The London depicted is not glamorous, but neither is it a city of mean and miserable streets. There is however, I think, a muted overarching melancholy. It's got something to do with the softness of the light, the general absence of harsh shadows and sharp contrasts. The tonal palette is reminiscent of work by photographers Bernd and Hilla Becher, which Berris acknowledges as an influence, though I'd say his approach is rather more humane and less systematic than theirs. Berris Conolly is not, in the usual sense, a 'street photographer', although the

majority of images here are taken in one street or another.

But we generally think of street photographers taking candid, even surreptitious pictures of the urban scene and its people – and it's hard to hide your intentions when you're using a fairly large medium-format camera and tripod. This means that, with a few exceptions, most of the people in them are well aware of the camera and the photographer. In some cases (the road sweeper) Berris asked them to pose, in other cases (the man with the goldfish) they saw his tripod set up and asked that he take their picture. Neither is Berris, strictly speaking, a landscape photographer although he certainly photographs landscapes and cityscapes. Perhaps the most satisfactory description of him is a 'documentarian'.

A timeline for London in the period these photographs were taken might well highlight three election wins for Margaret Thatcher, the Falklands conflict, the marriage of Charles and Diana, the spread of AIDS, the Brixton riots, IRA bombs in Hyde Park and Regent's Park. History is not absent from these photographs – how could it be? The billboard 'inviting' you to the christening of Prince William could be dated within a week, but history exists as a background, a given. No doubt some of the people in the photographs voted for Thatcher and some may have gone on marches against her, some perhaps were fans of Kylie Minogue, some of Guns N' Roses, but that's not what defines them. The era is not limited in that way.

These photographs show streets where people are quietly getting on with their lives, not oblivious to what's happening around them, but with their own private, domestic concerns and priorities. They are documents, not news flashes. There is an undercurrent of change: a boarded-up business, tower blocks being demolished, Shoreditch station being overtaken by nature, the petrol station in King's Cross that now looks so retro must once have seemed so futuristic. But some things hardly change at all. That image of the South Bank, or the Natural History Museum, or Abney Park Cemetery, could have been taken yesterday. There's a lot to look at in these photographs, and inevitably the more you look the more you see – a process Berris calls 'density of reference'. And there are some surprises, such as the 'Too Much Ozone' graffiti in Ada Street, which seems to have been way ahead of the game. Did people really worry about ozone in the 80s? I never met anybody who did.

Note the shop in Rushmore Road with the conspicuous Hovis sign, then below it the hand-painted words 'English and West Indian'. This surely says something about race relations, but it does so quietly, inconspicuously. And isn't it amazing, and a sign of how some things persist, that there's a sticker saying 'Murdoch is bad news' in the rear window of that car on Bakers Hill? Sometimes there's a mystery that can't be solved, such as the row of first aid boxes on a shelf behind the chickens hung up in Ridley Road market. Was somebody anticipating a lot of accidents, or did they just collect them? And exactly what kind of place was the Tudor Café in Oldhill Street? It looks like it can't have held more than three people at the best of times. Yes, these photographs speak for themselves, but sometimes they don't tell you everything you'd like to know. Life's like that. After you've spent some time looking at them, you may walk down the street and find yourself stepping into Conolly's London.

Geoff Nicholson, 2021

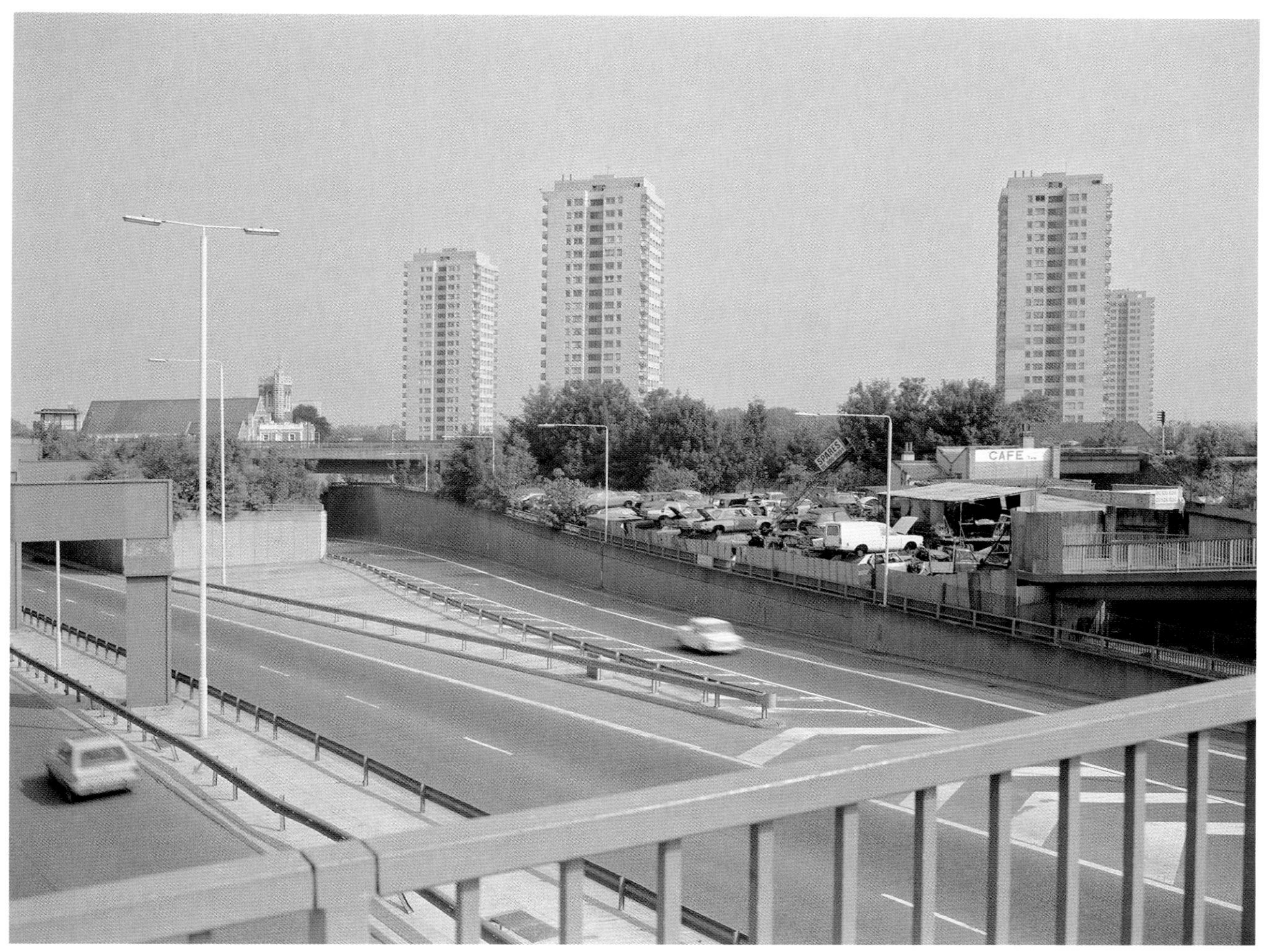

A102M and Trowbridge Estate E9, 1986

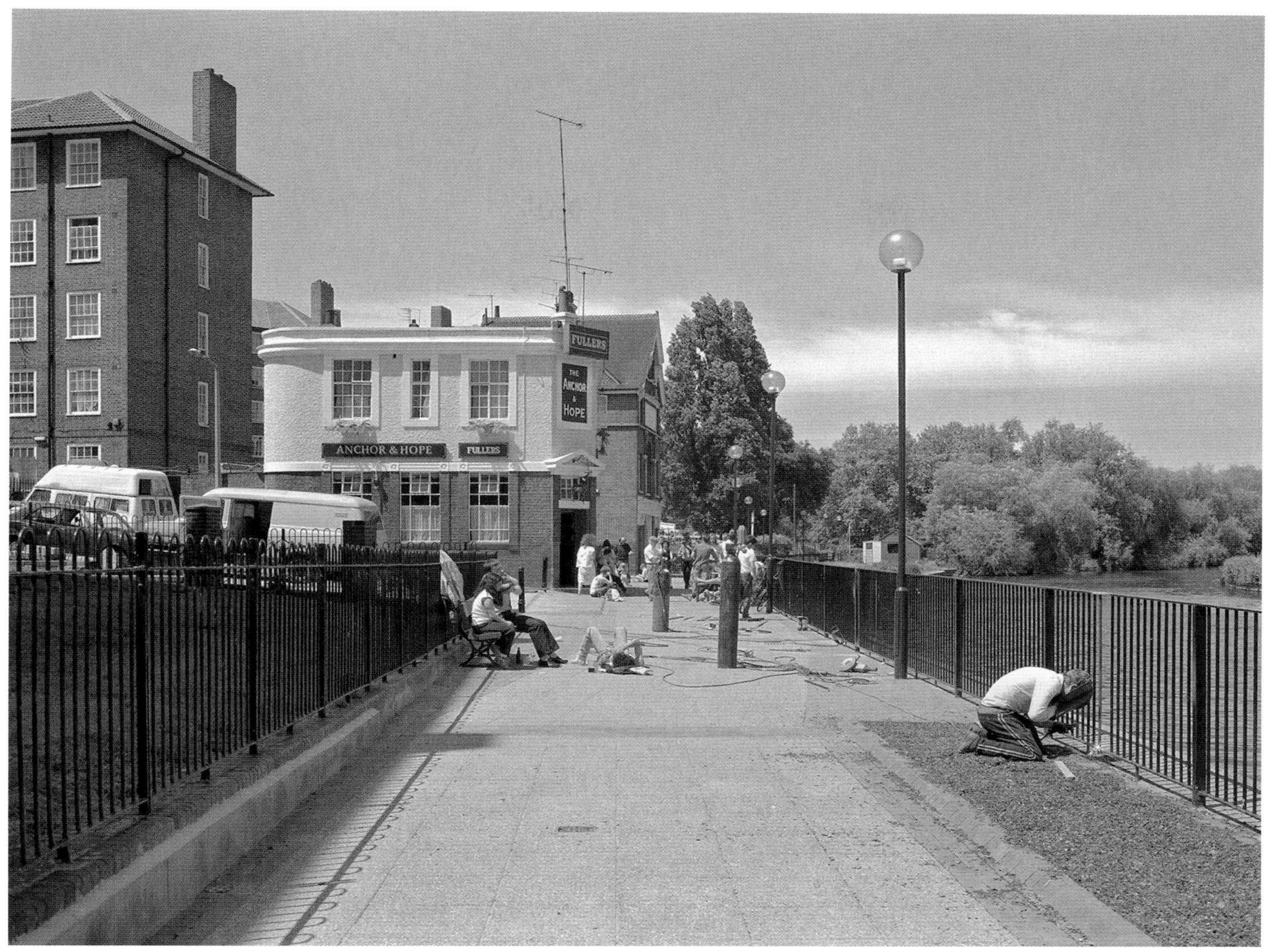

High Hill Ferry E5, 1986

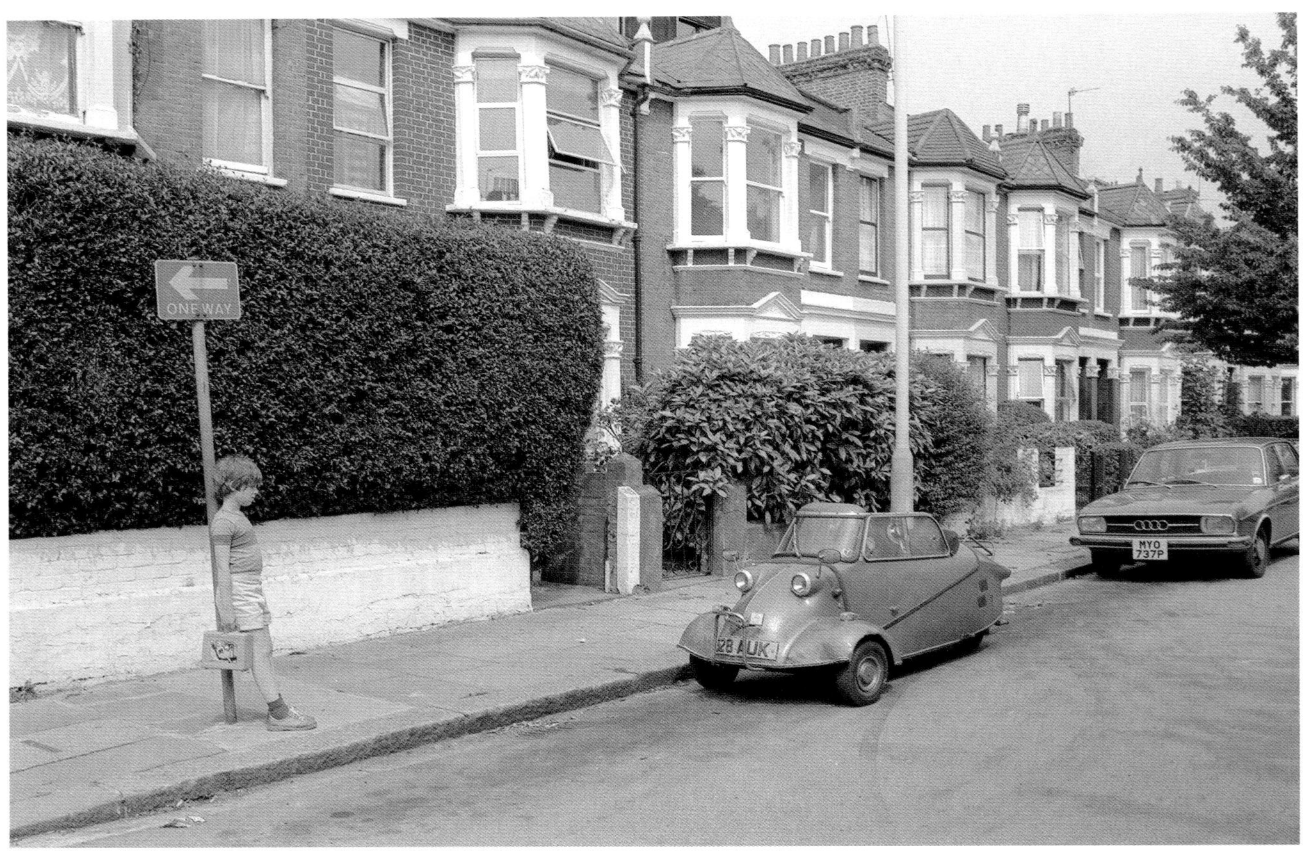

unrecorded location, 1979

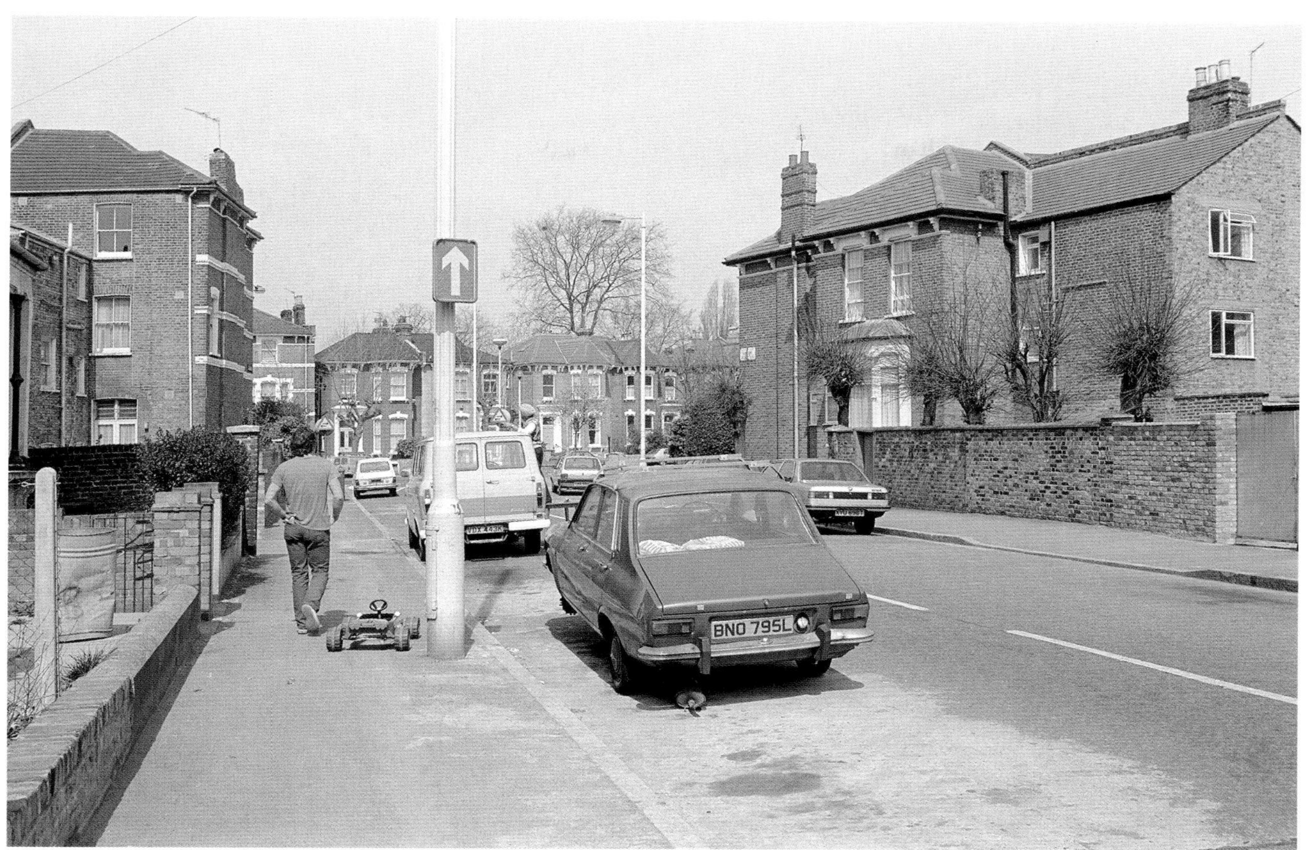

Maury Road N16, 1984

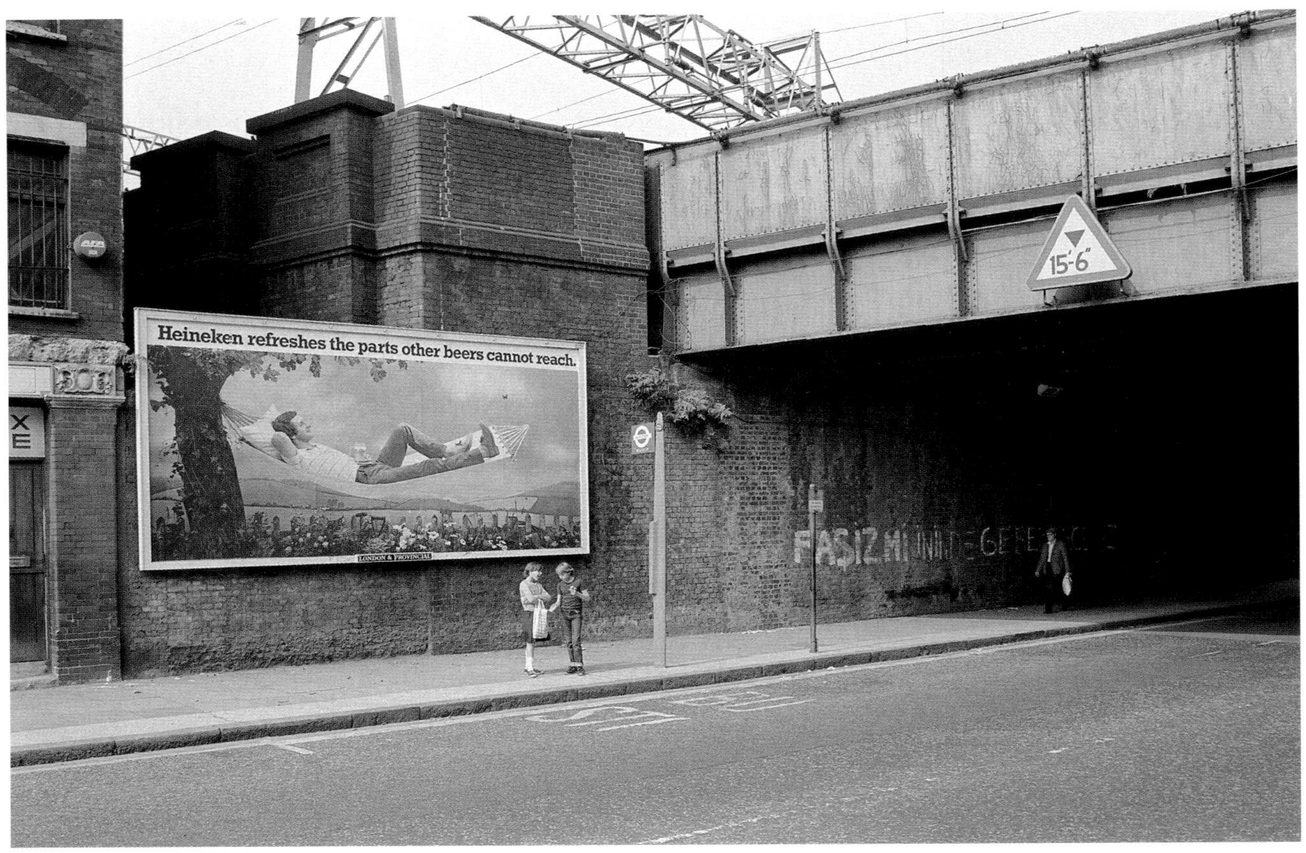

Cambridge Heath Road E2, 1982

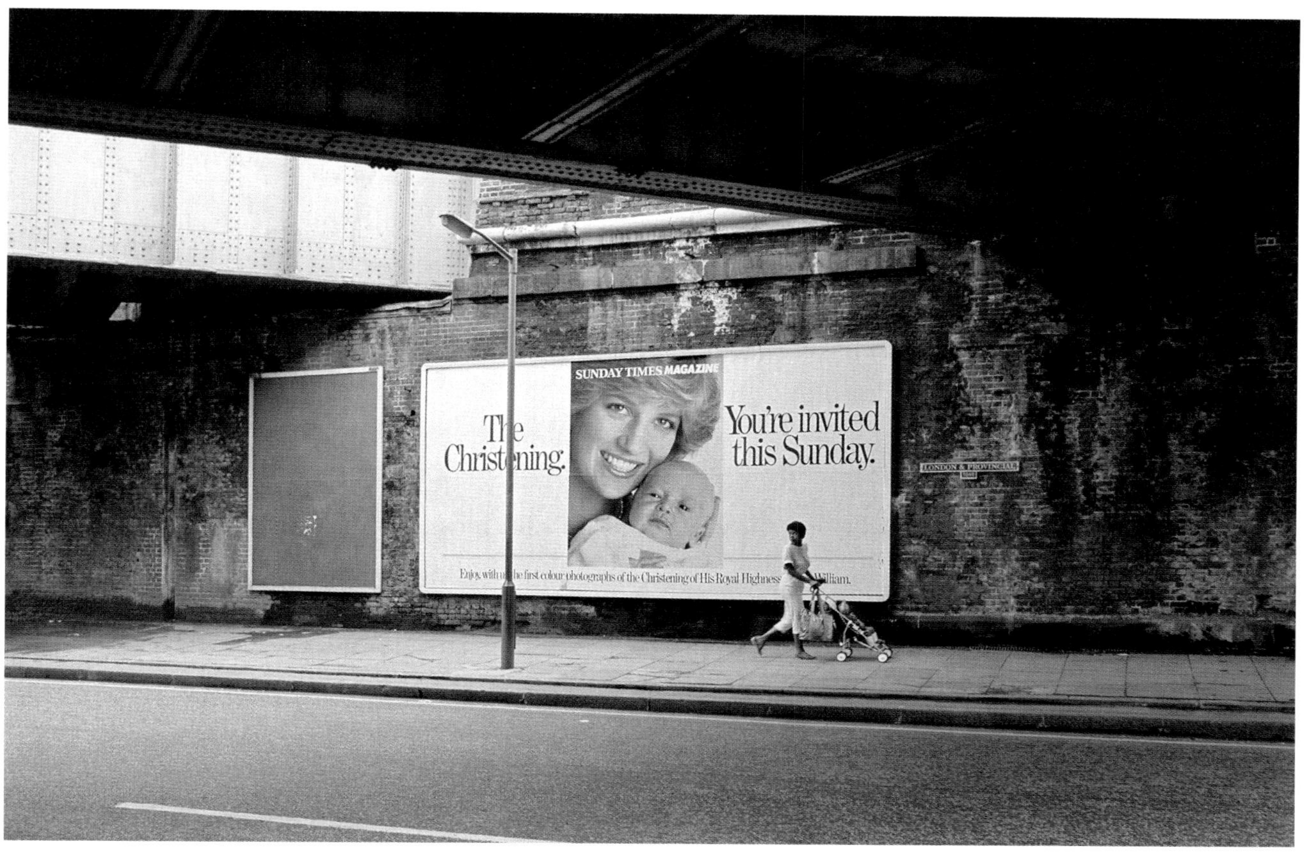

Seven Sisters Road N4, 1982

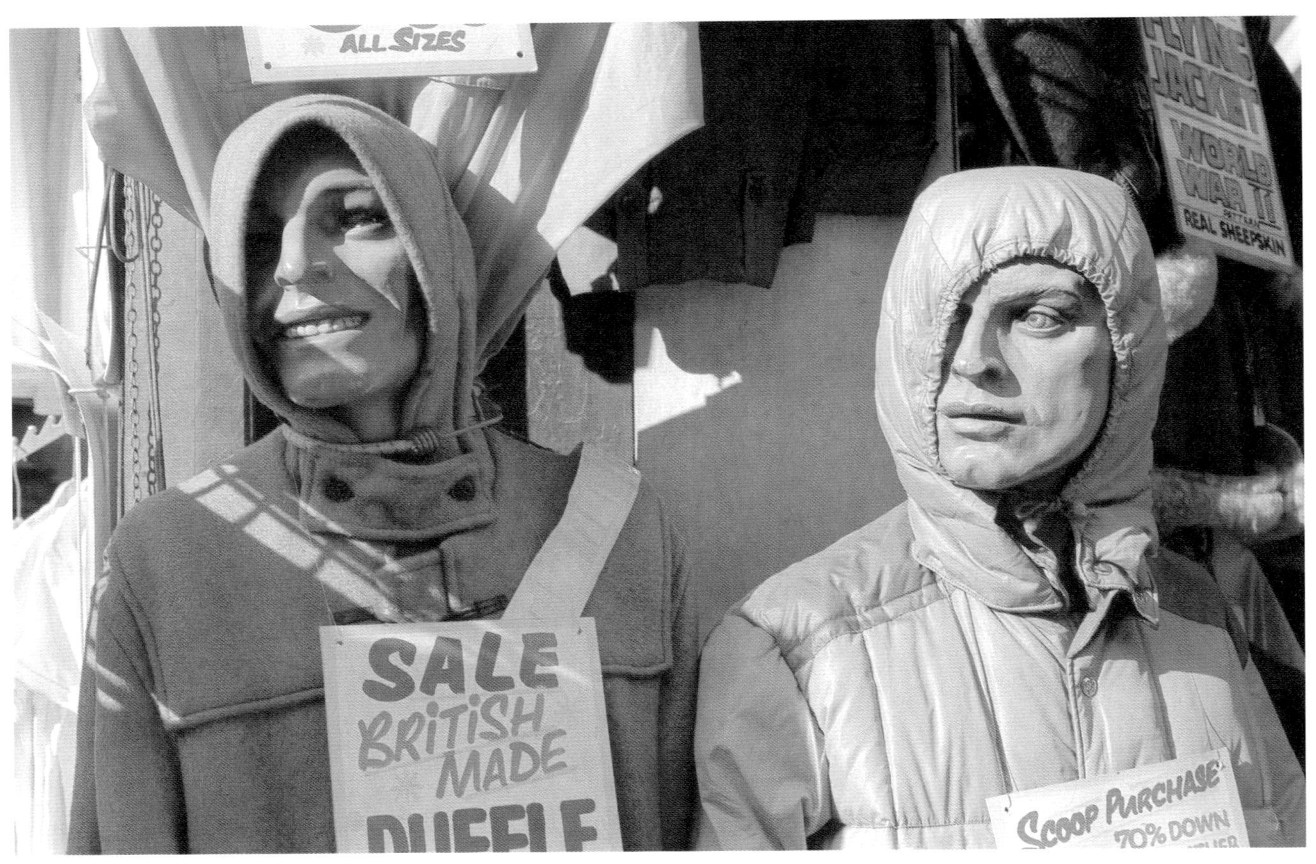

unrecorded location, 1981
(opposite) Crossway N16, 1982

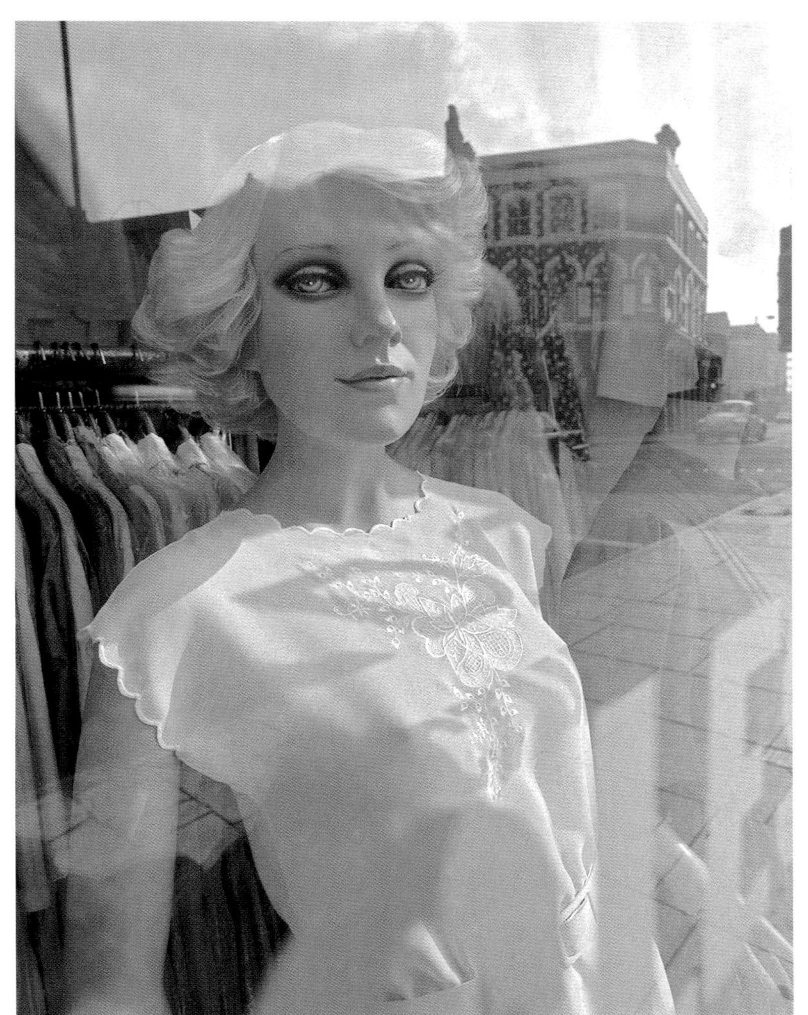

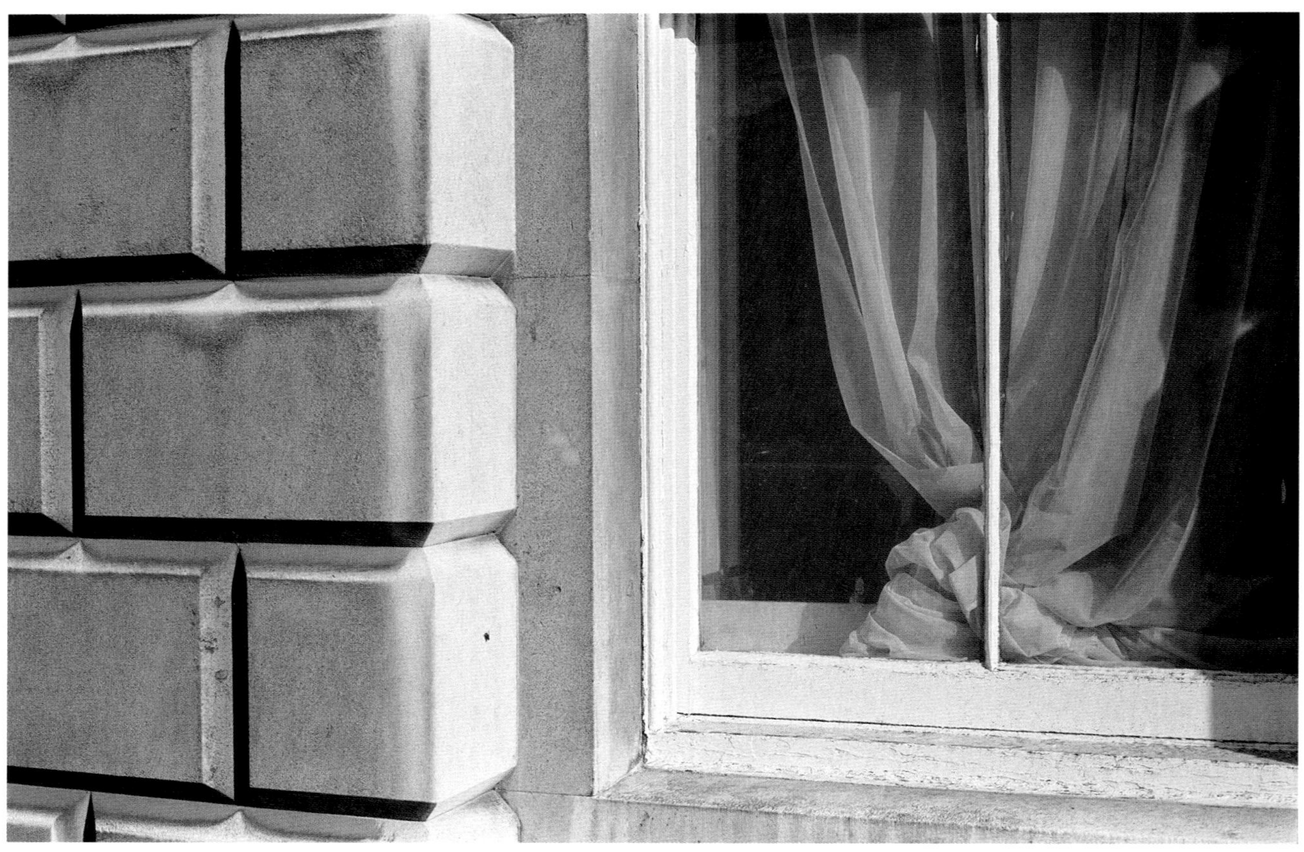

Somerset House WC2, 1983

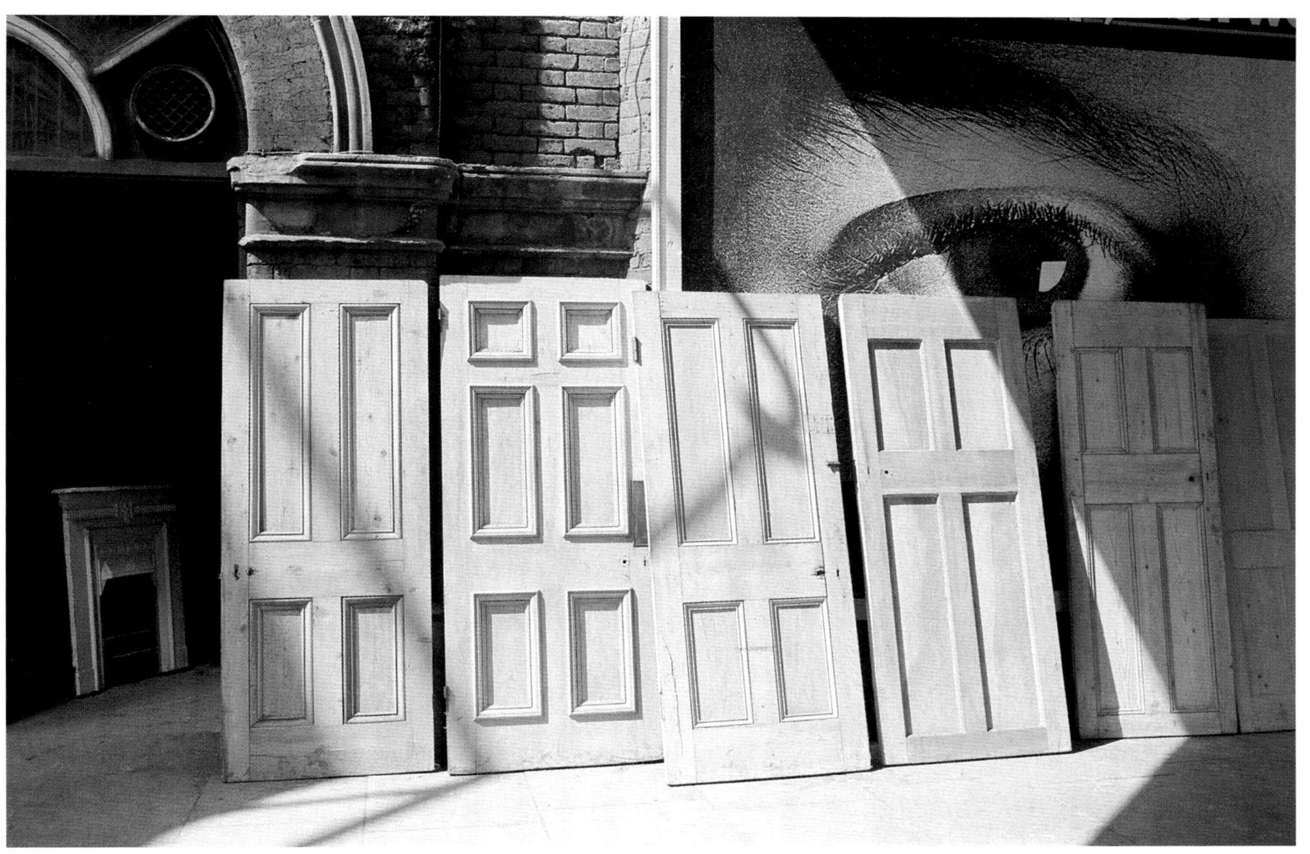

Camden Road Station NW1, 1982

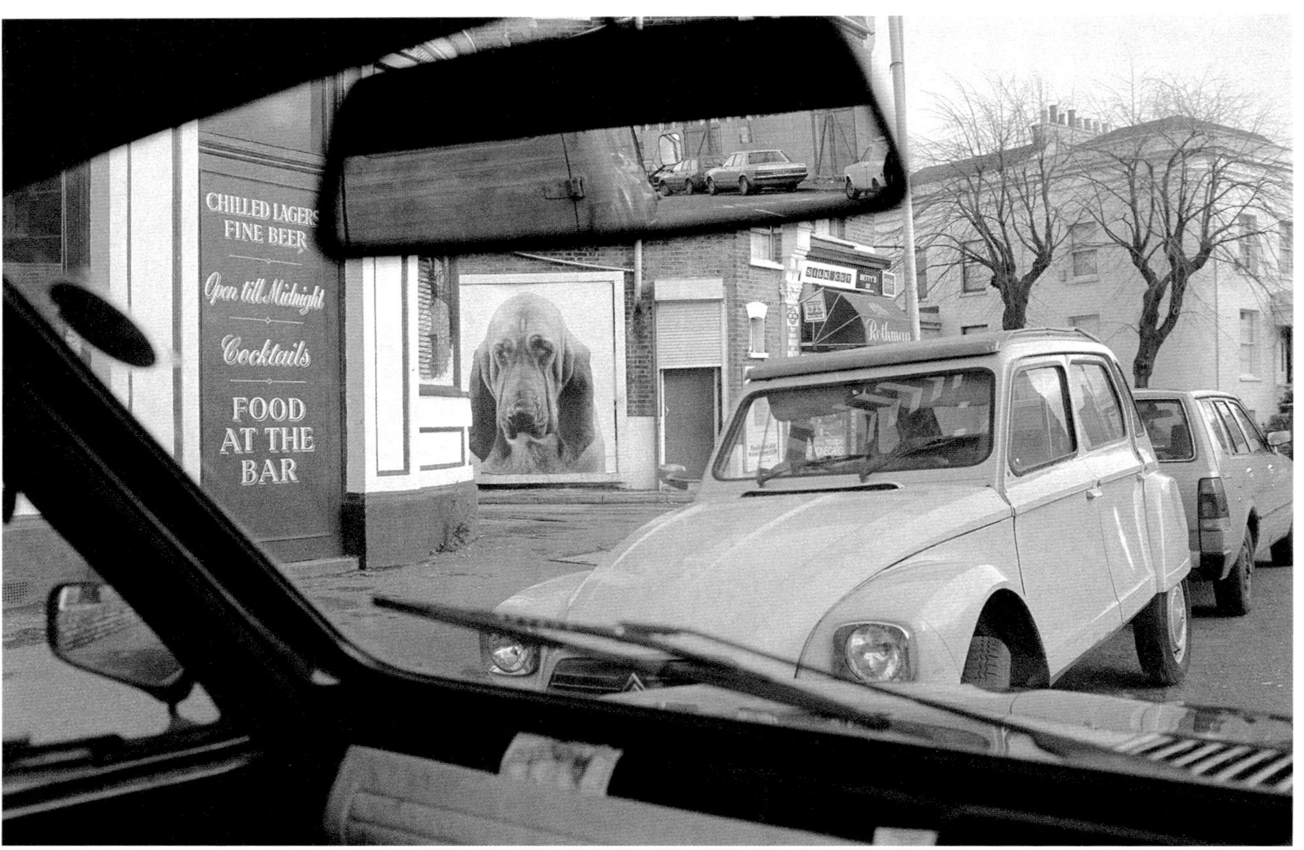

Clissold Road N16, 1987

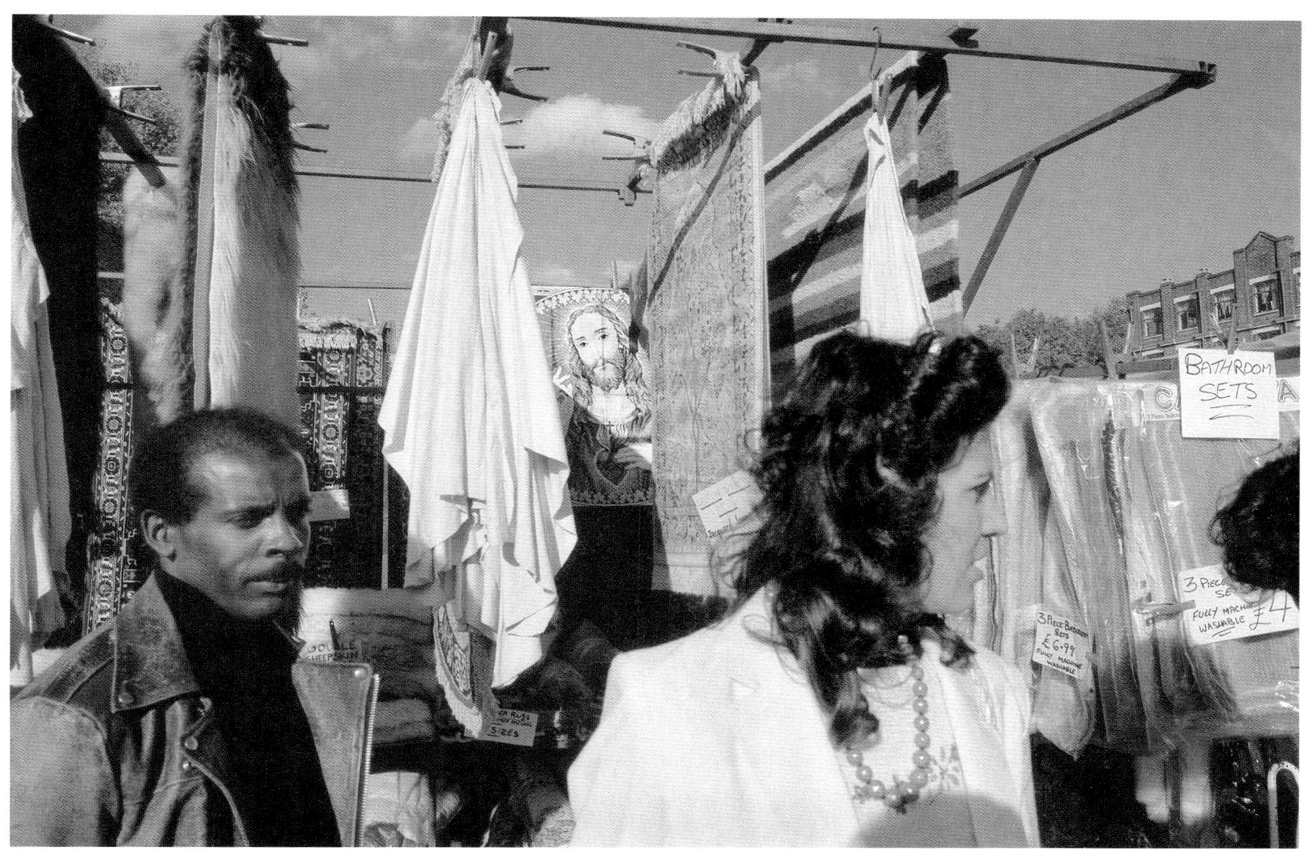

Ridley Road E8, 1984

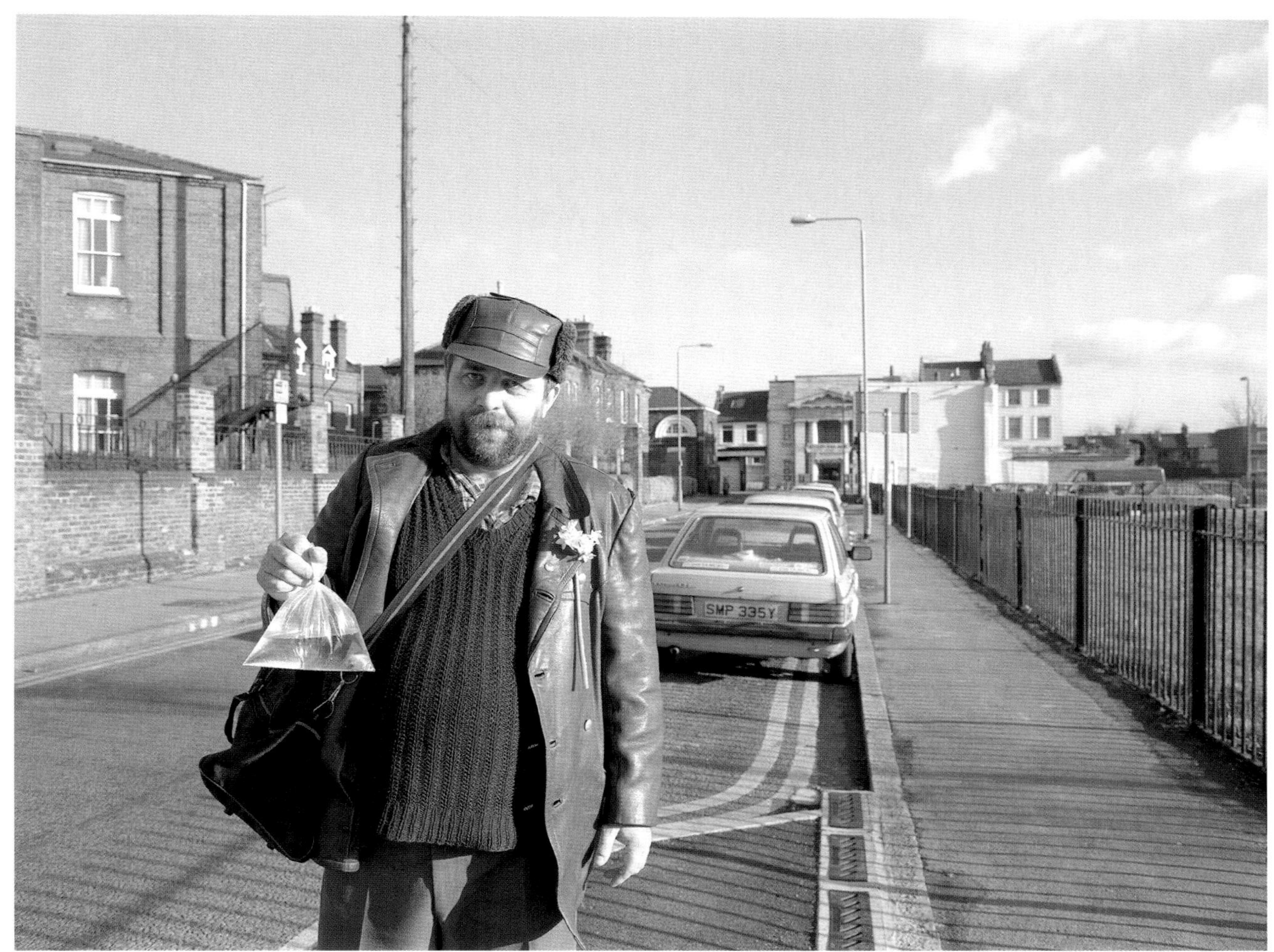

Homerton Grove E5, 1987

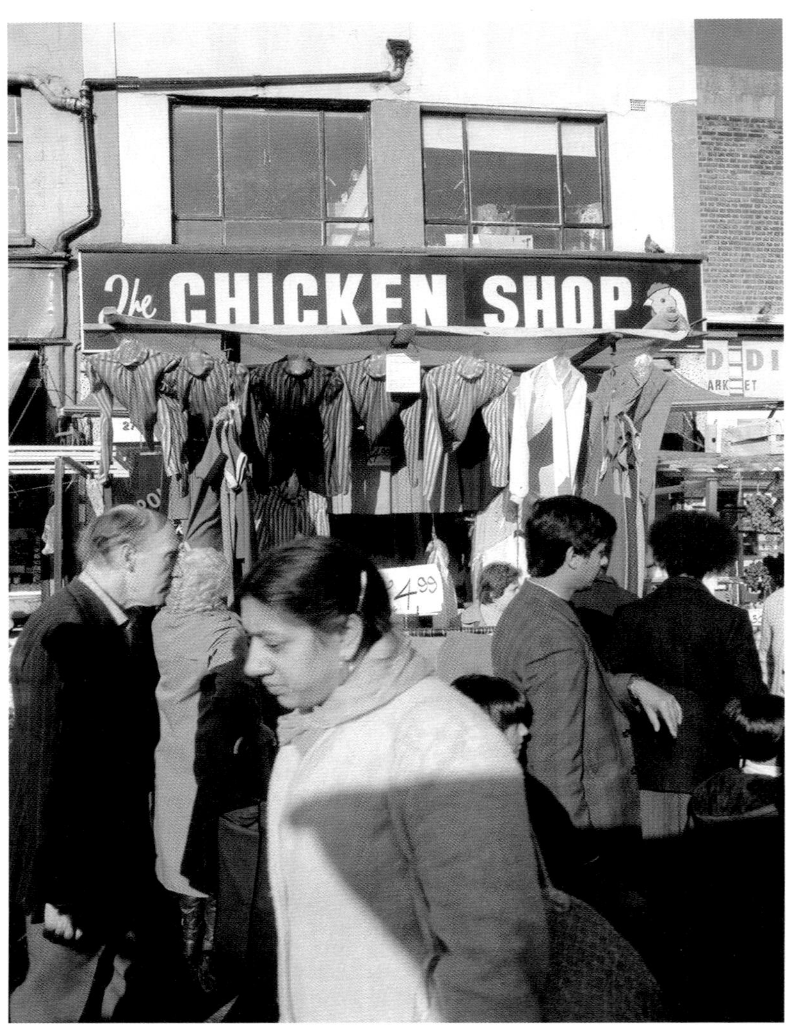

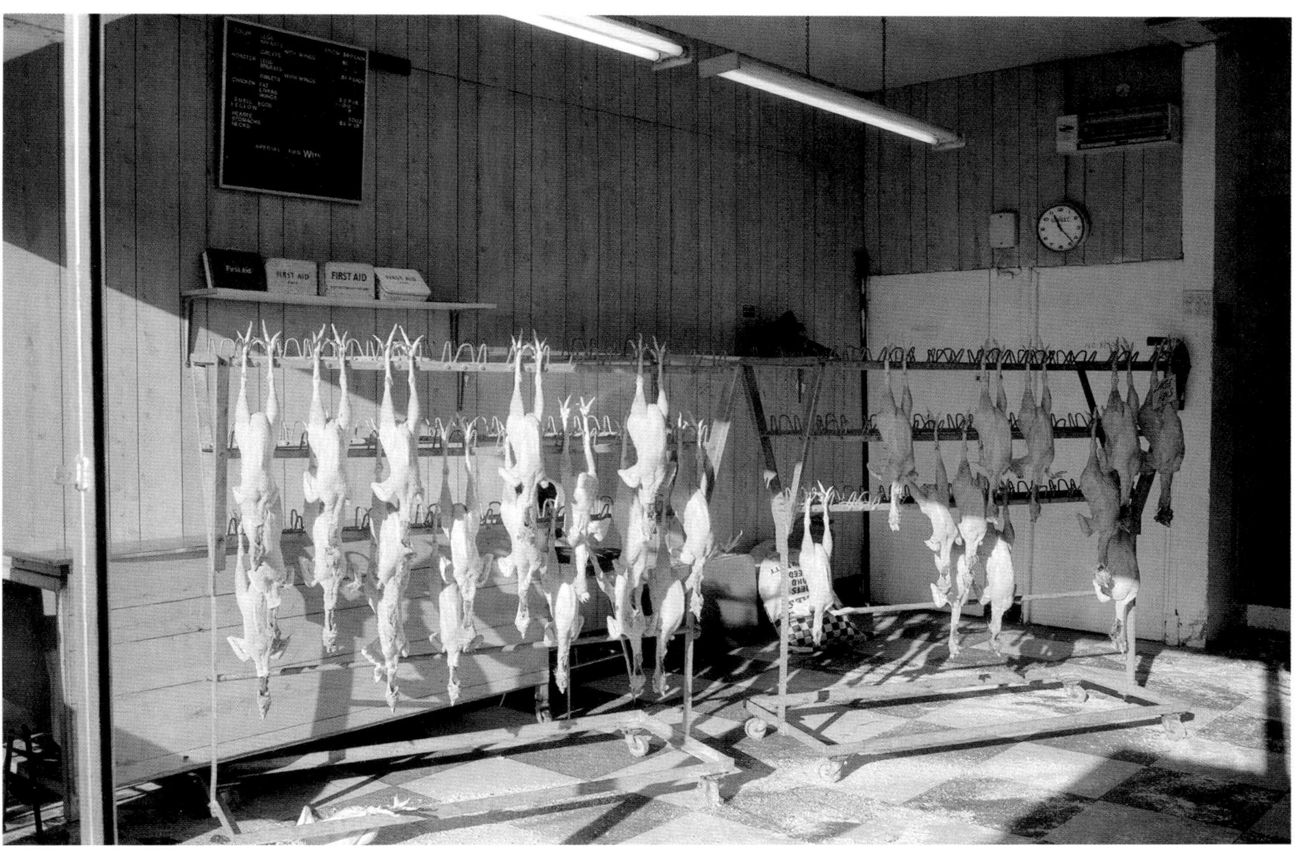

(*both*) Ridley Road E8, 1984

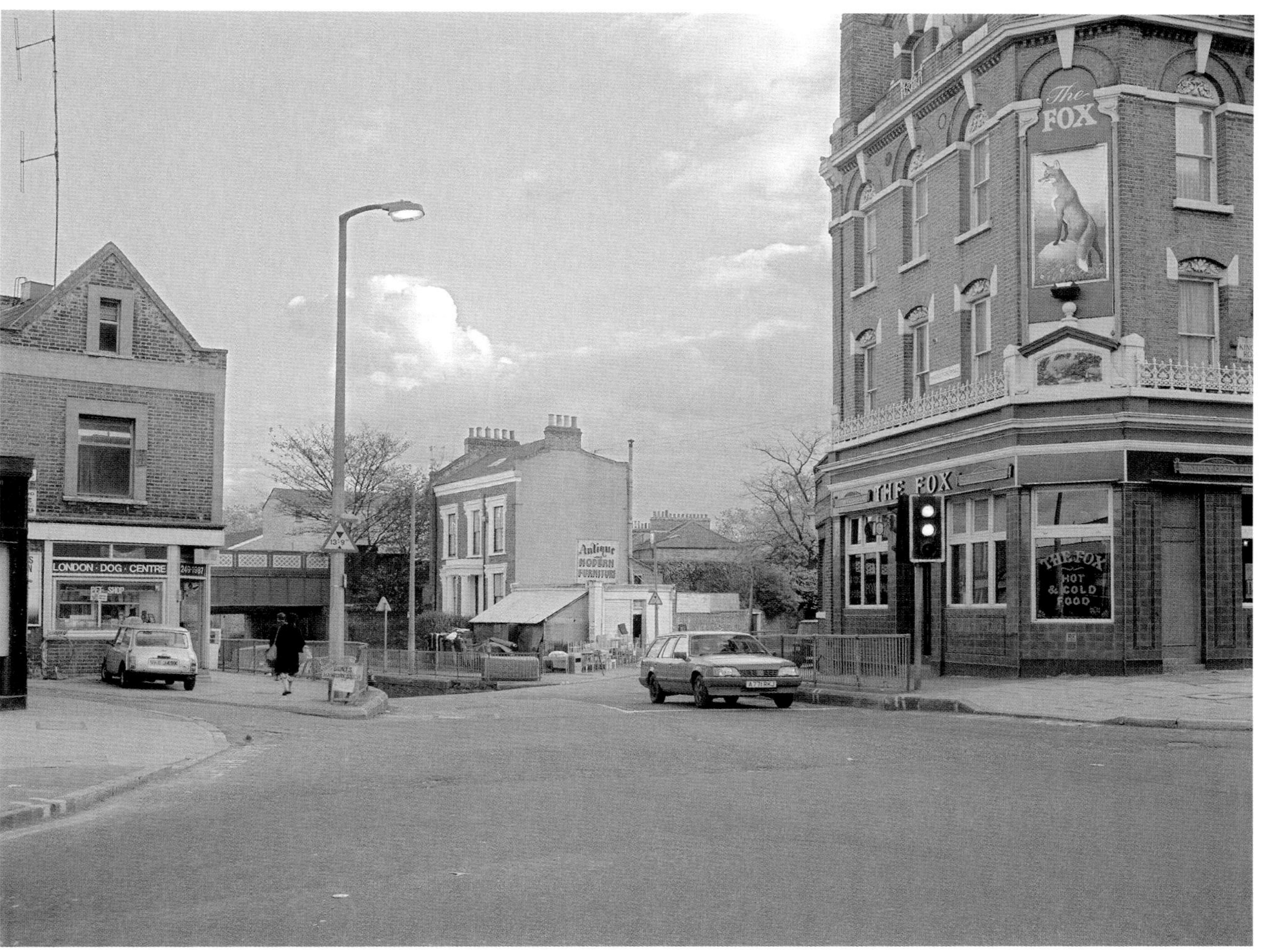

Kingsland Road E8, 1985

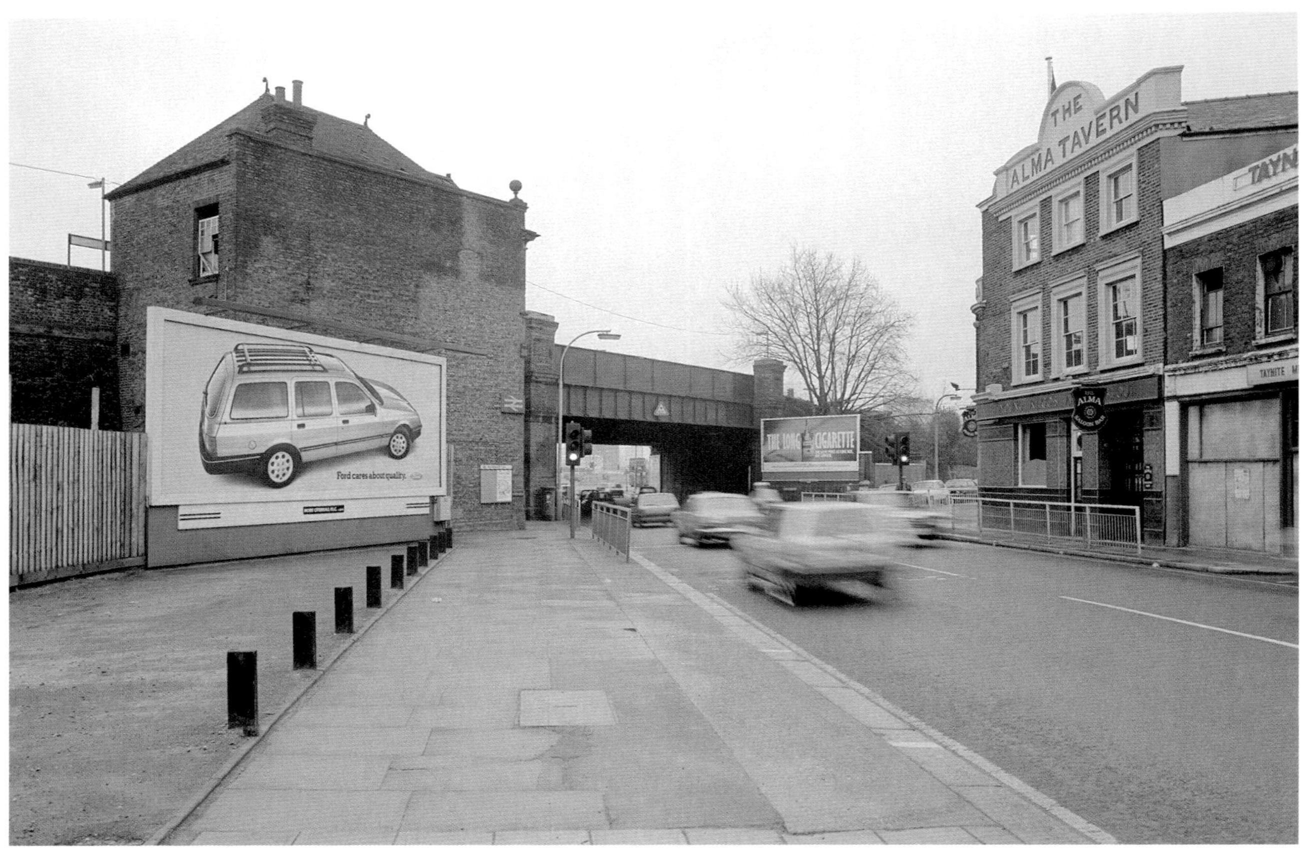

Old York Road SW18, 1983

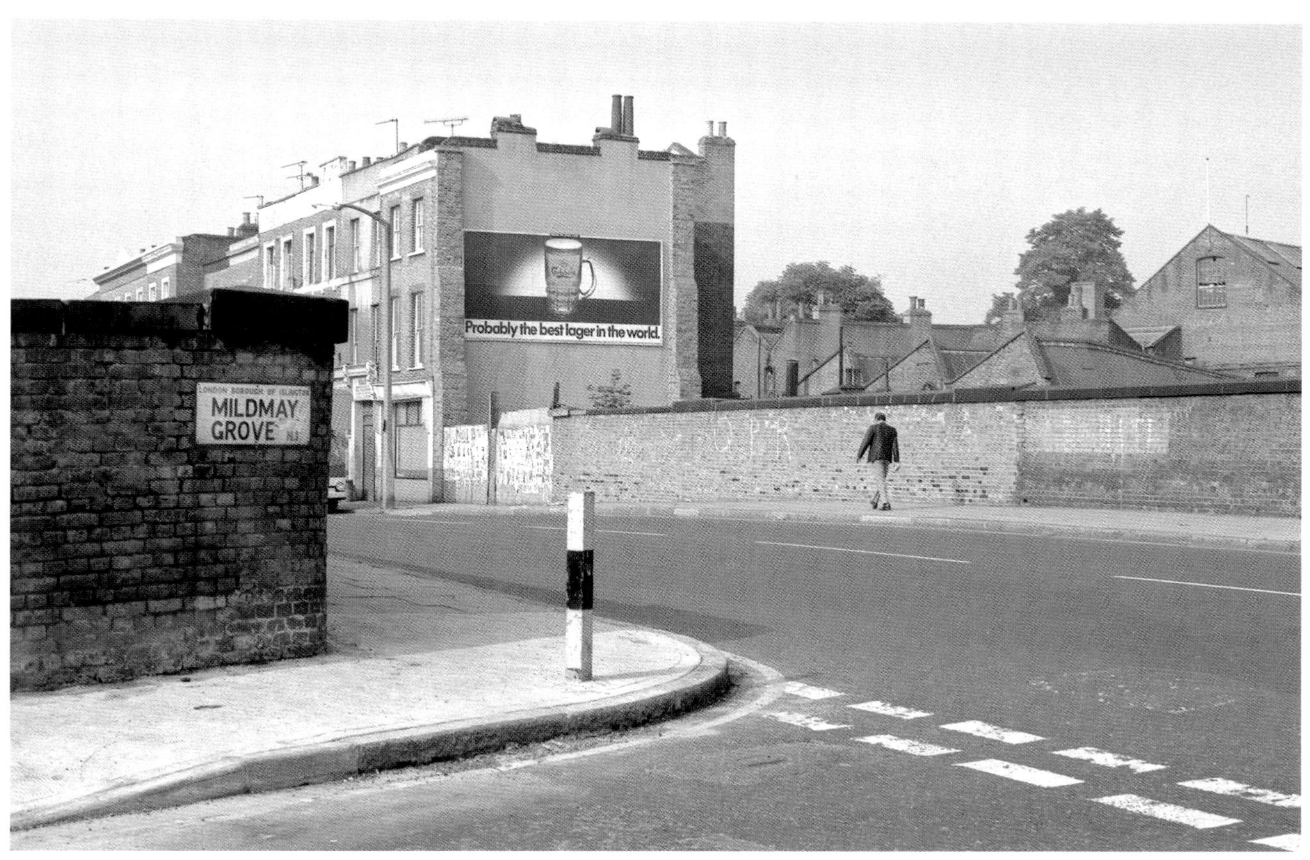

Mildmay Grove N1, 1981

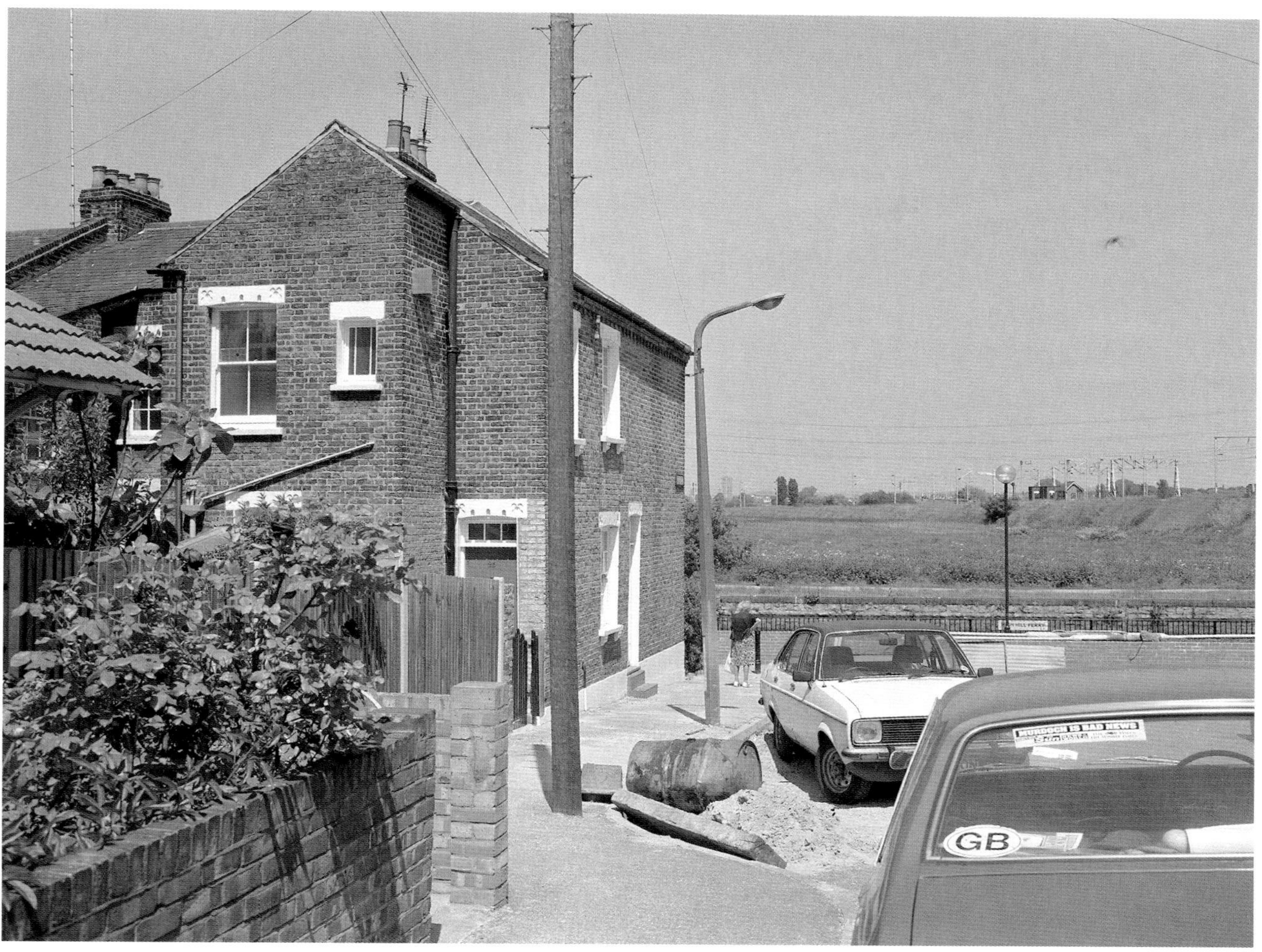

Bakers Hill E5, 1986

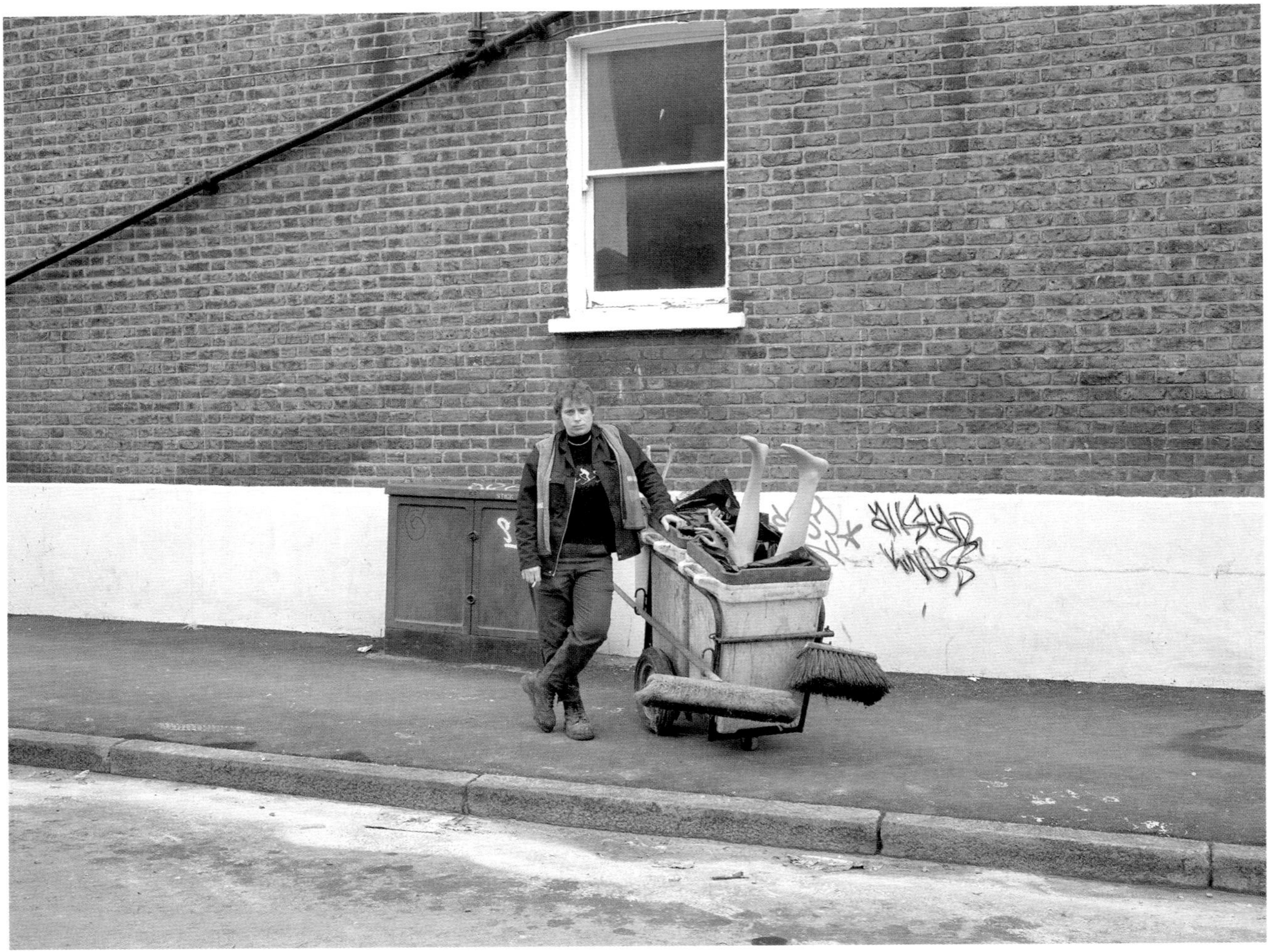

Maury Road N16, 1981

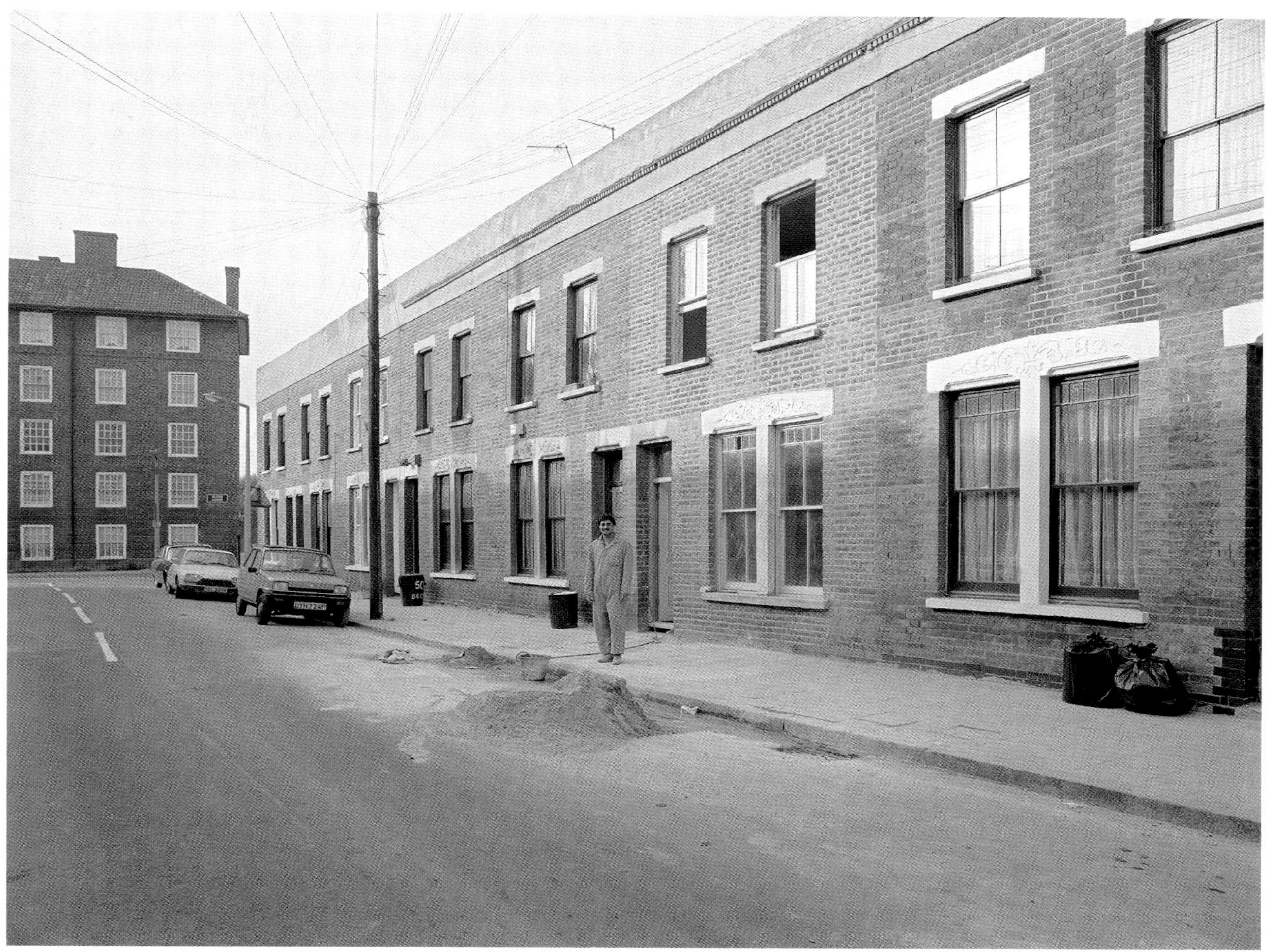

Beck Road E8, 1985

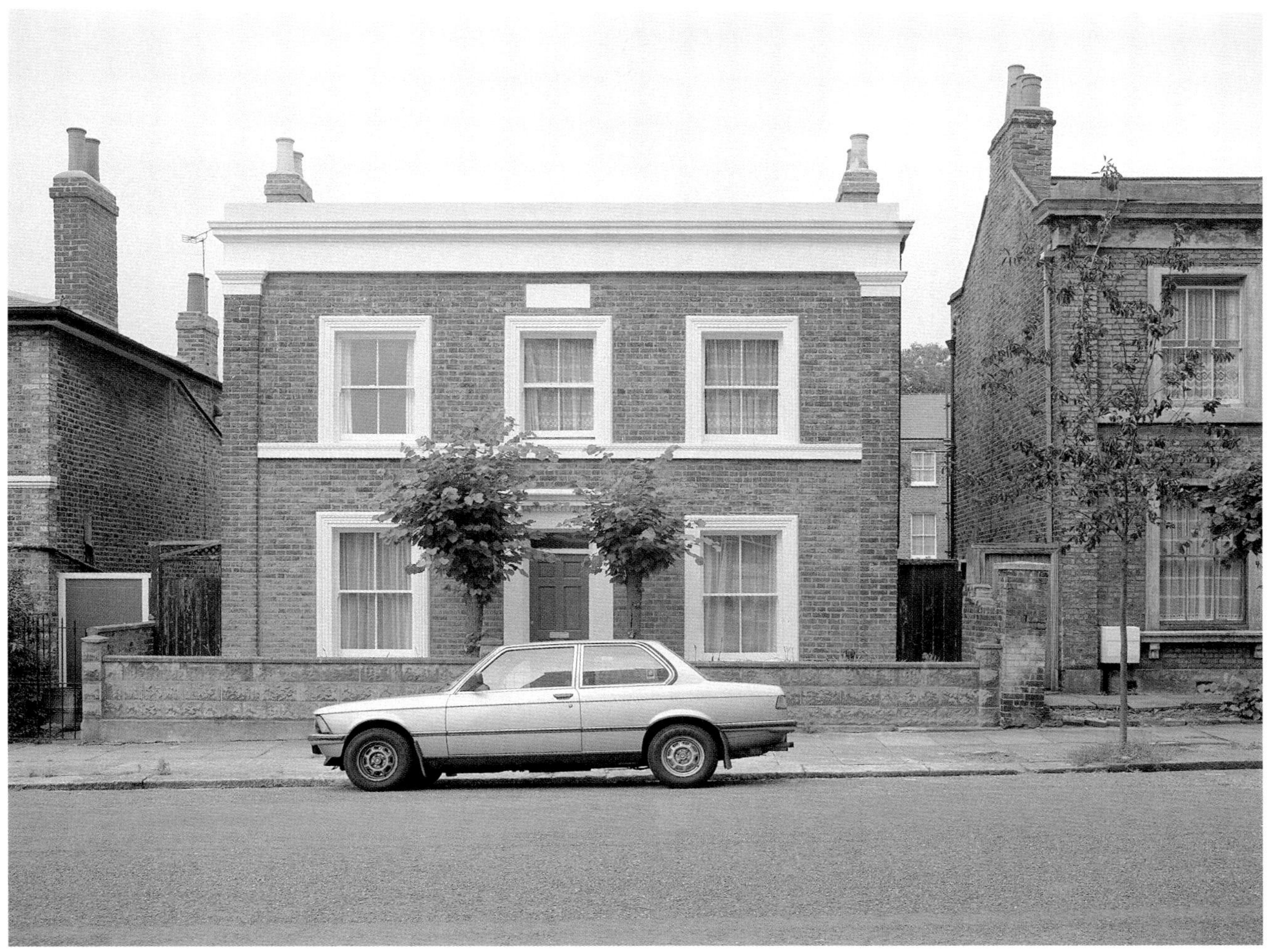

Yoakley Road N16, 1987

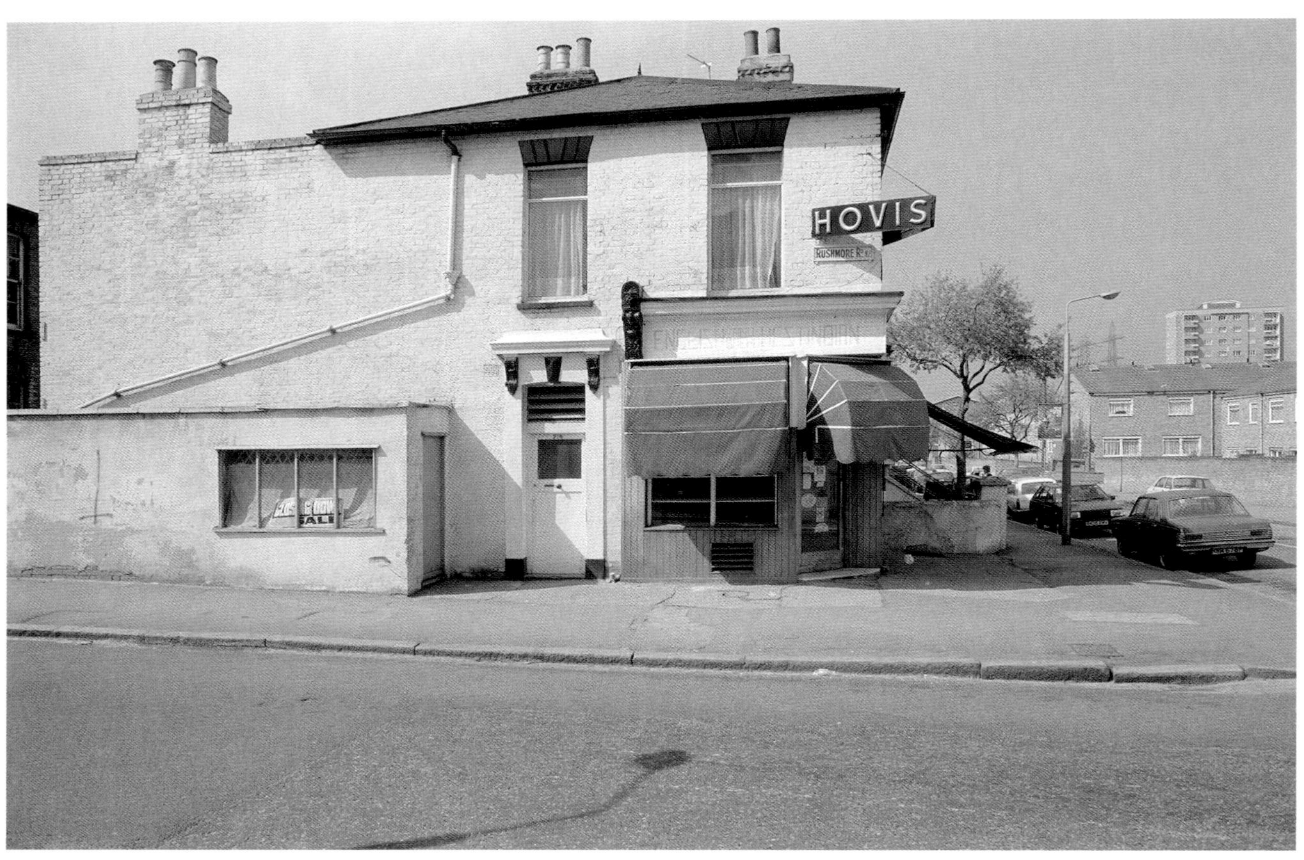

Rushmore Road E5, 1987

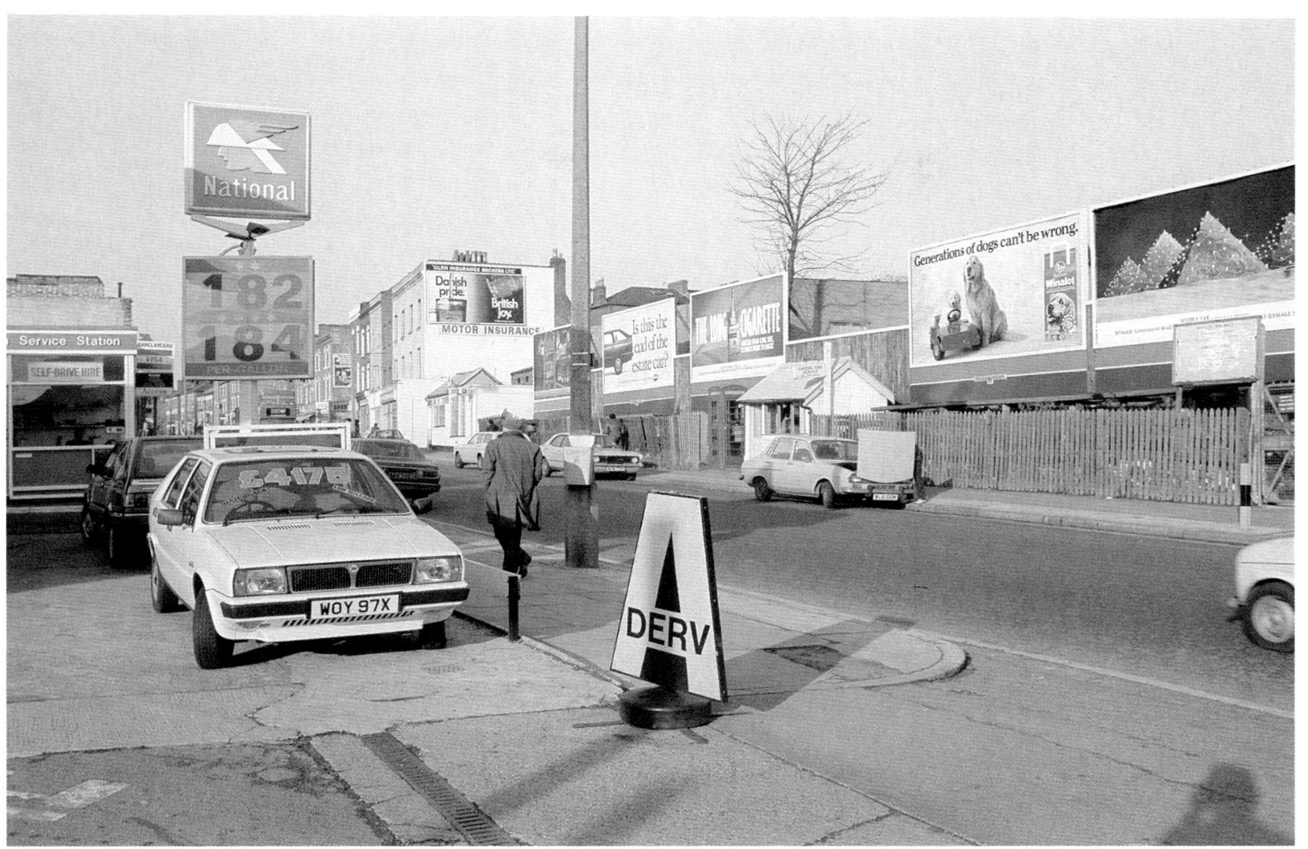

Stroud Green Road N4, 1984

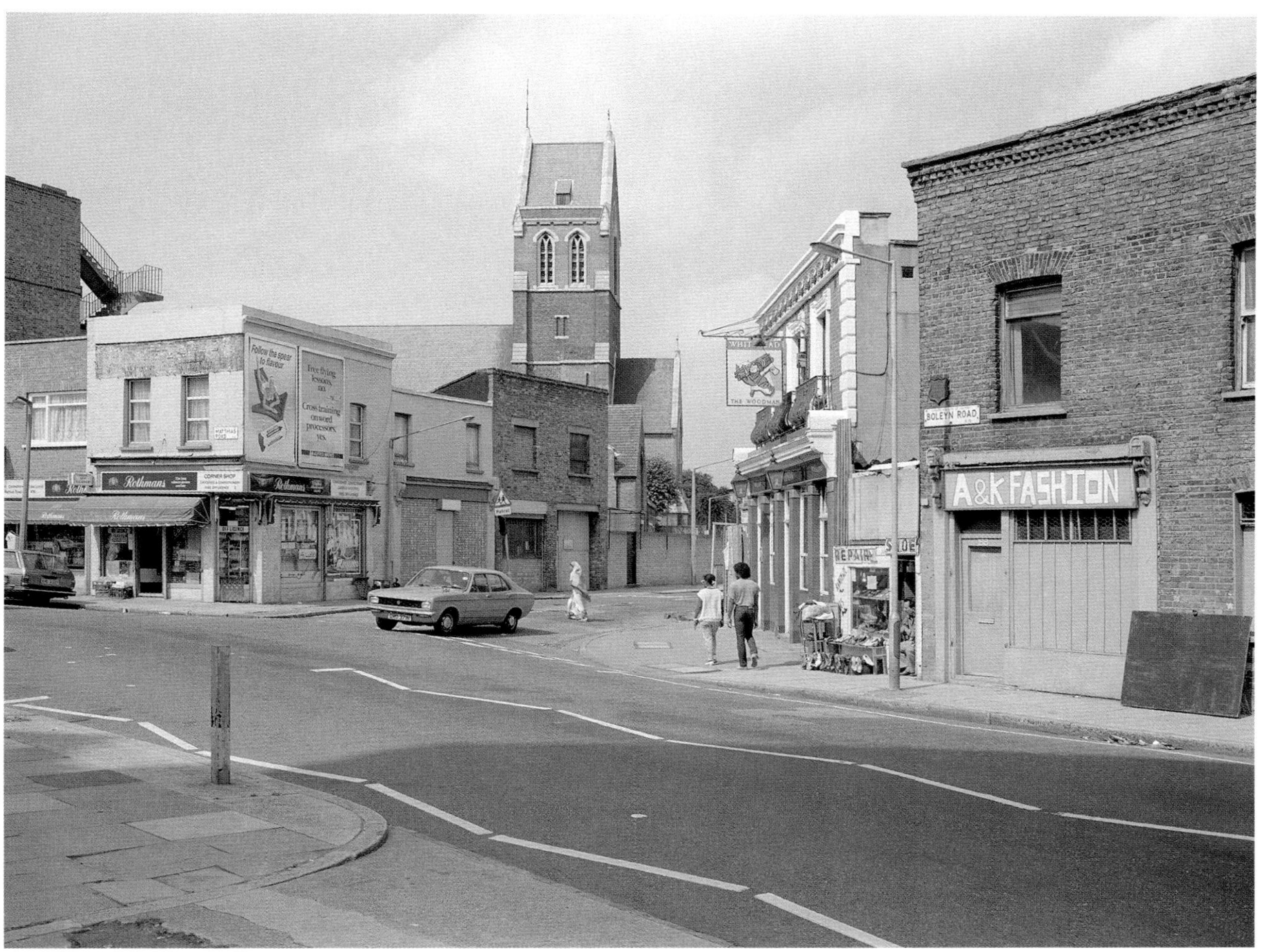

Boleyn Road N16, 1986

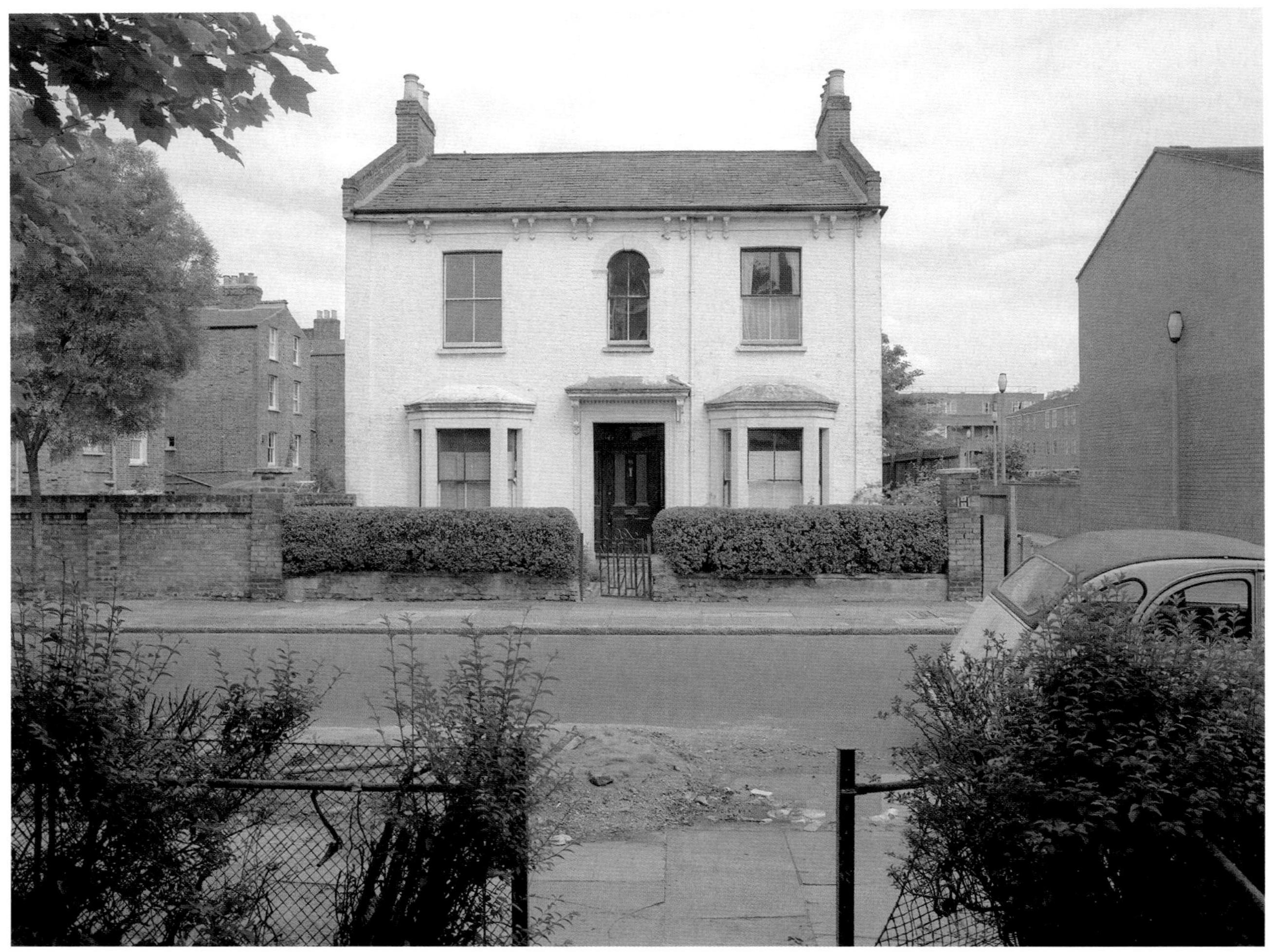

Lansdowne Drive E8, 1987

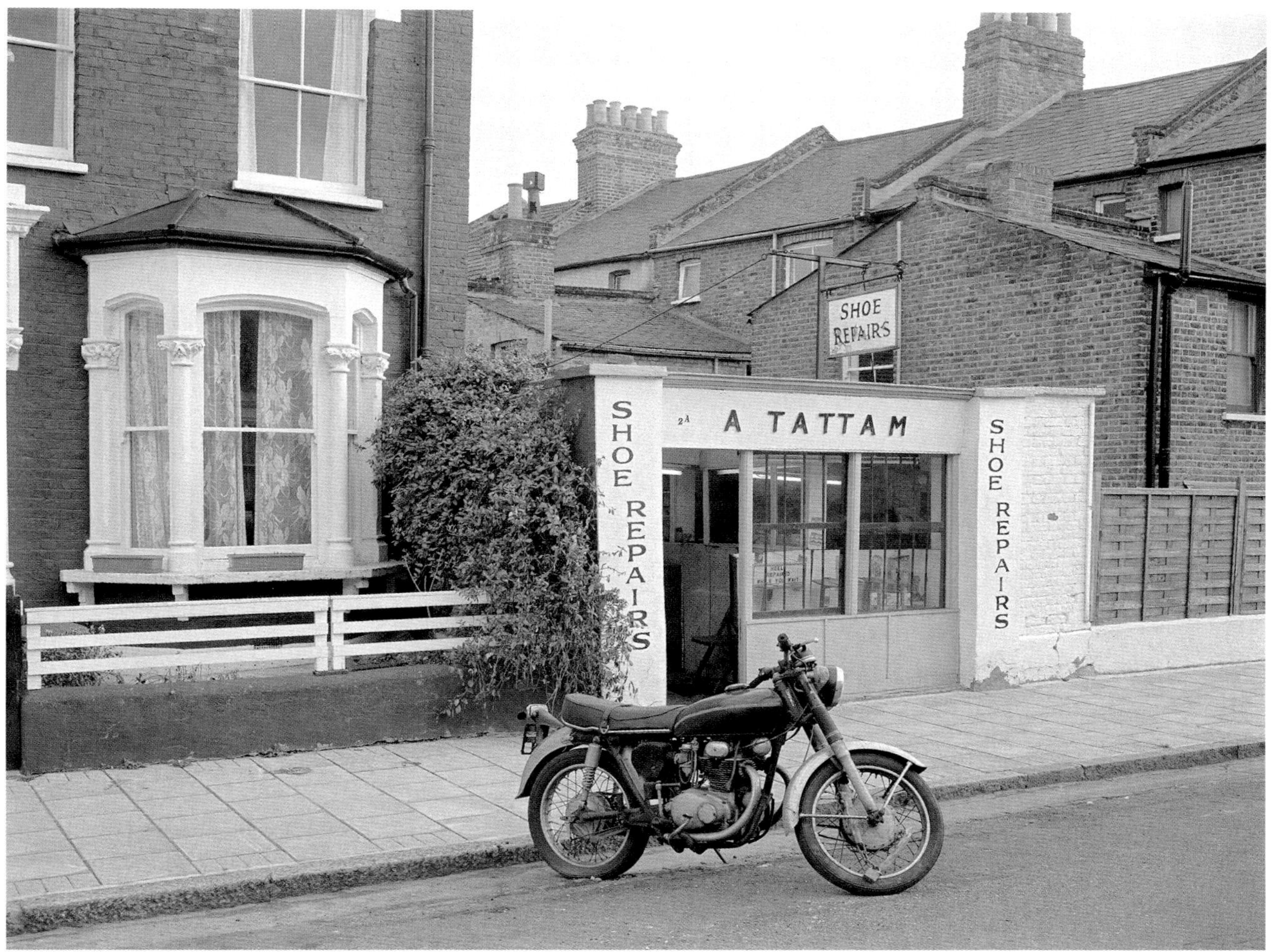

Brodia Road N16, 1986

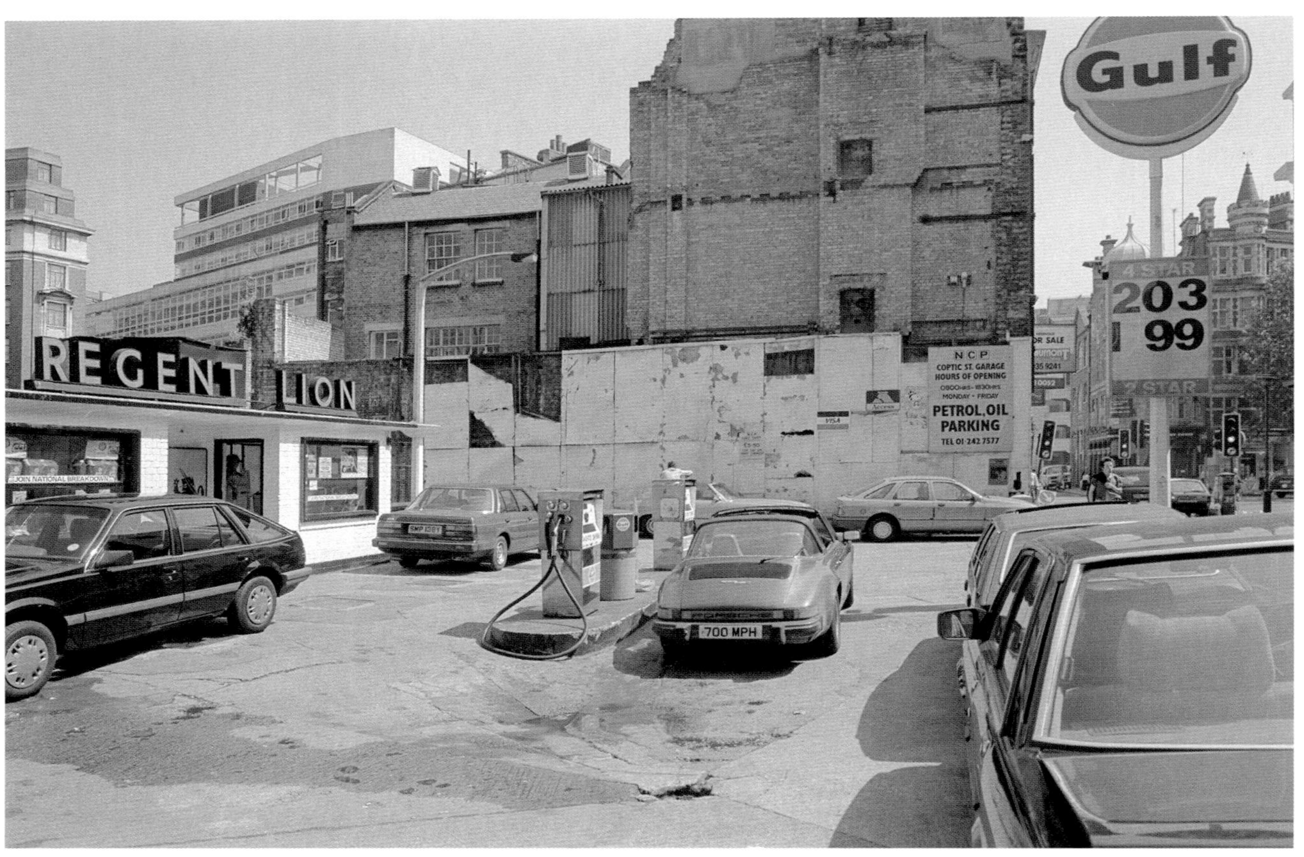

Coptic Street WC1, 1985

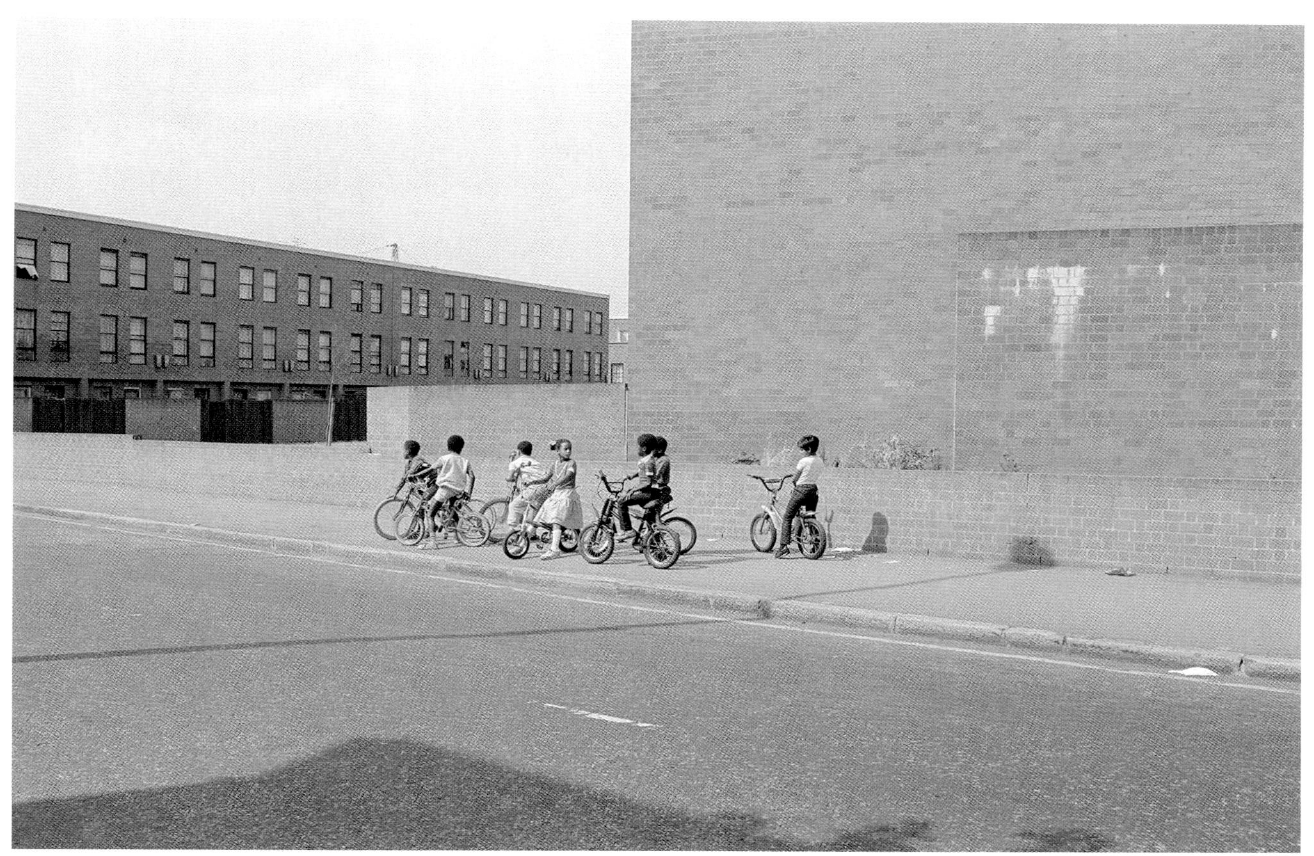

Brooke Road N16, 1983

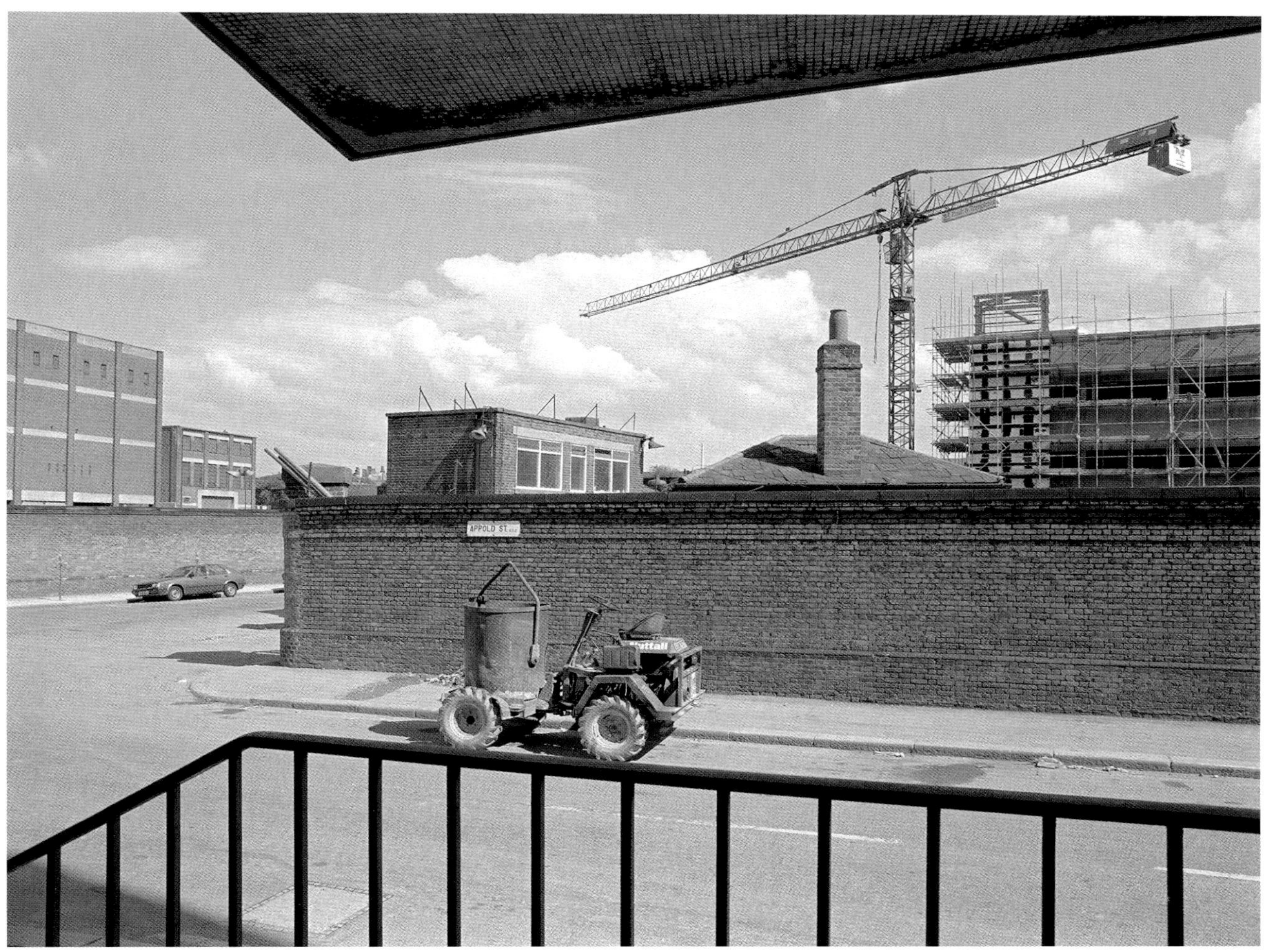

Appold Street EC2, 1987

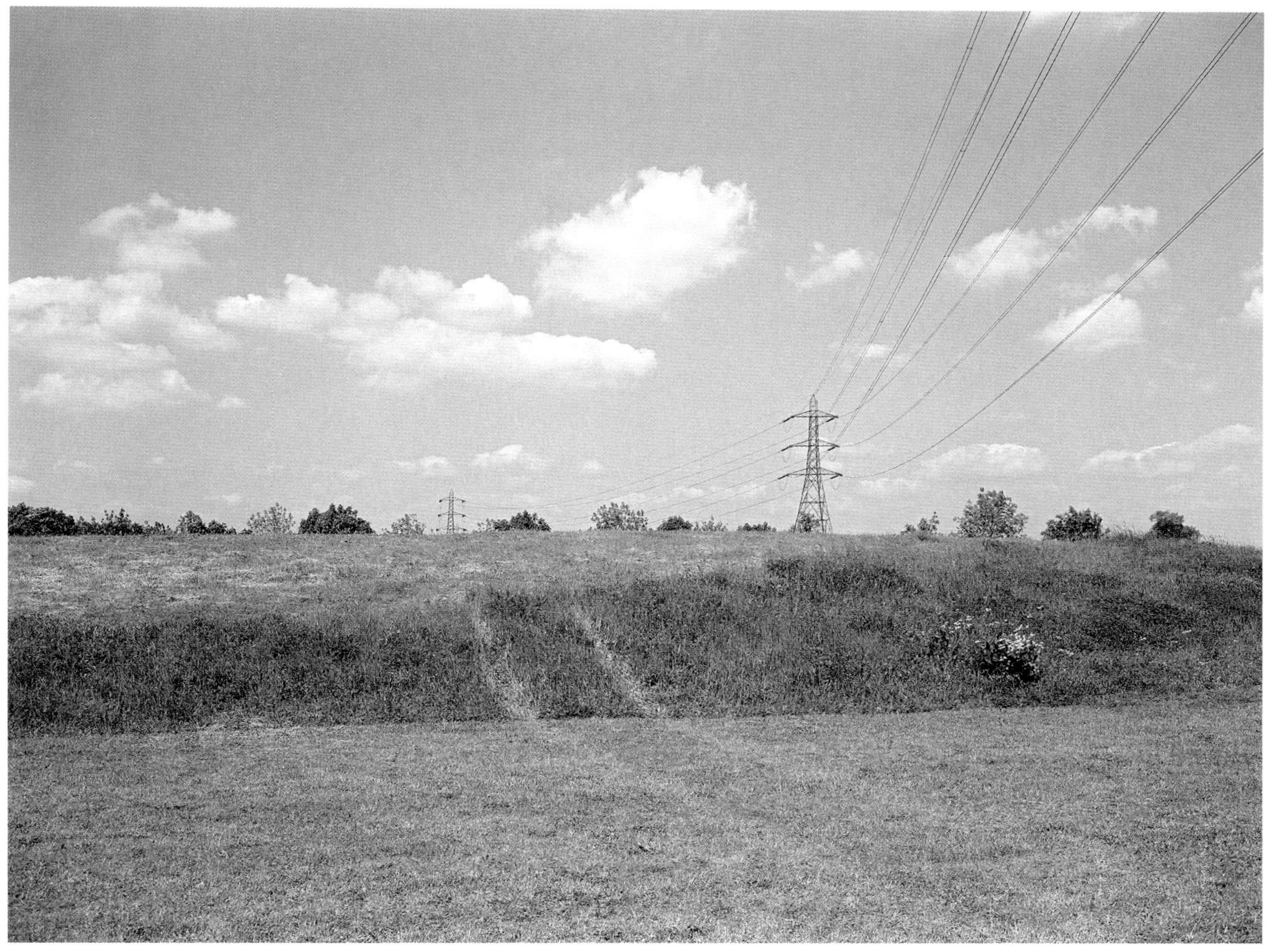

Lee Valley Park E17, 1985

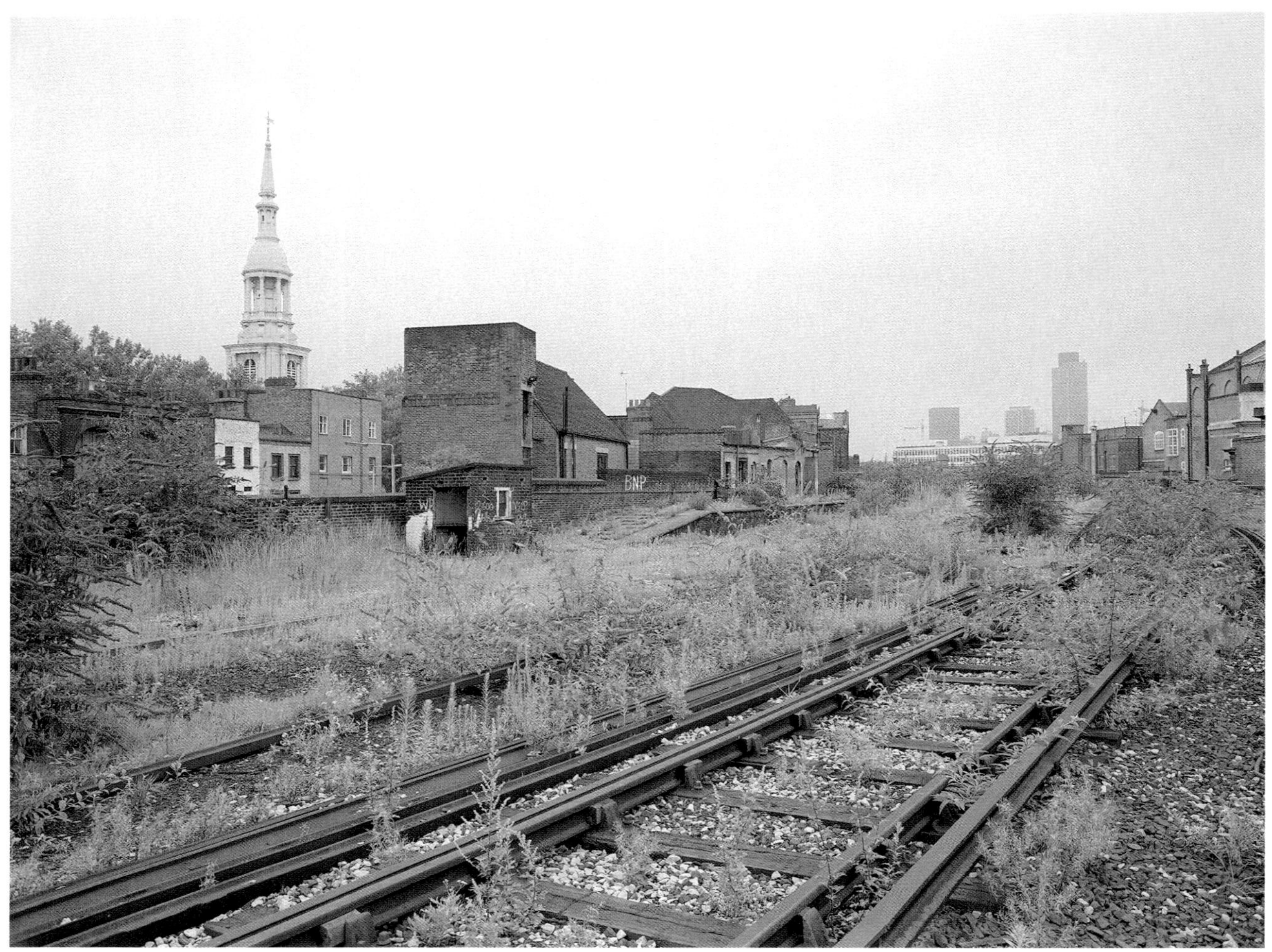

Shoreditch Station E2, 1987

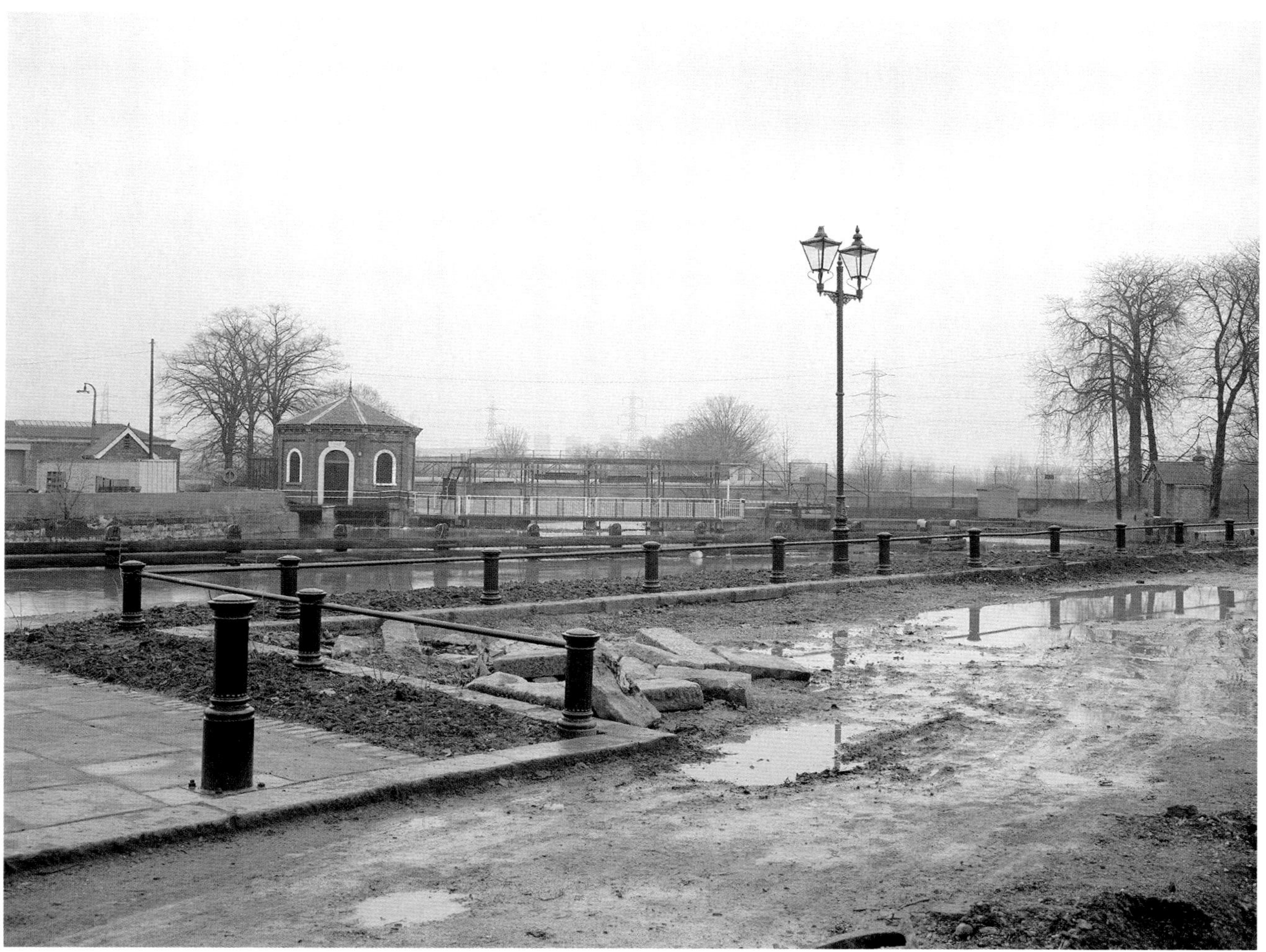

Waterworks Lane E5, 1985

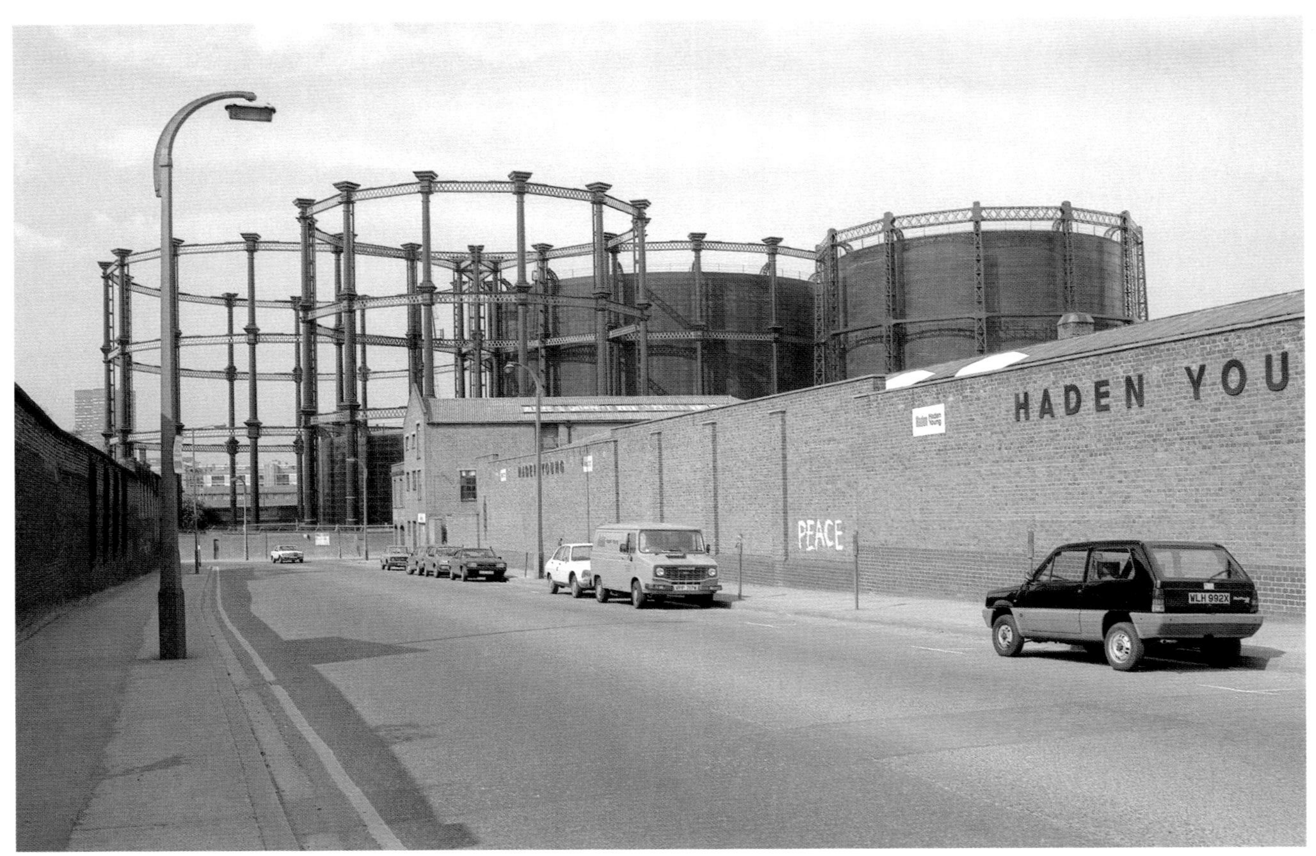

Goods Way N1, 1982

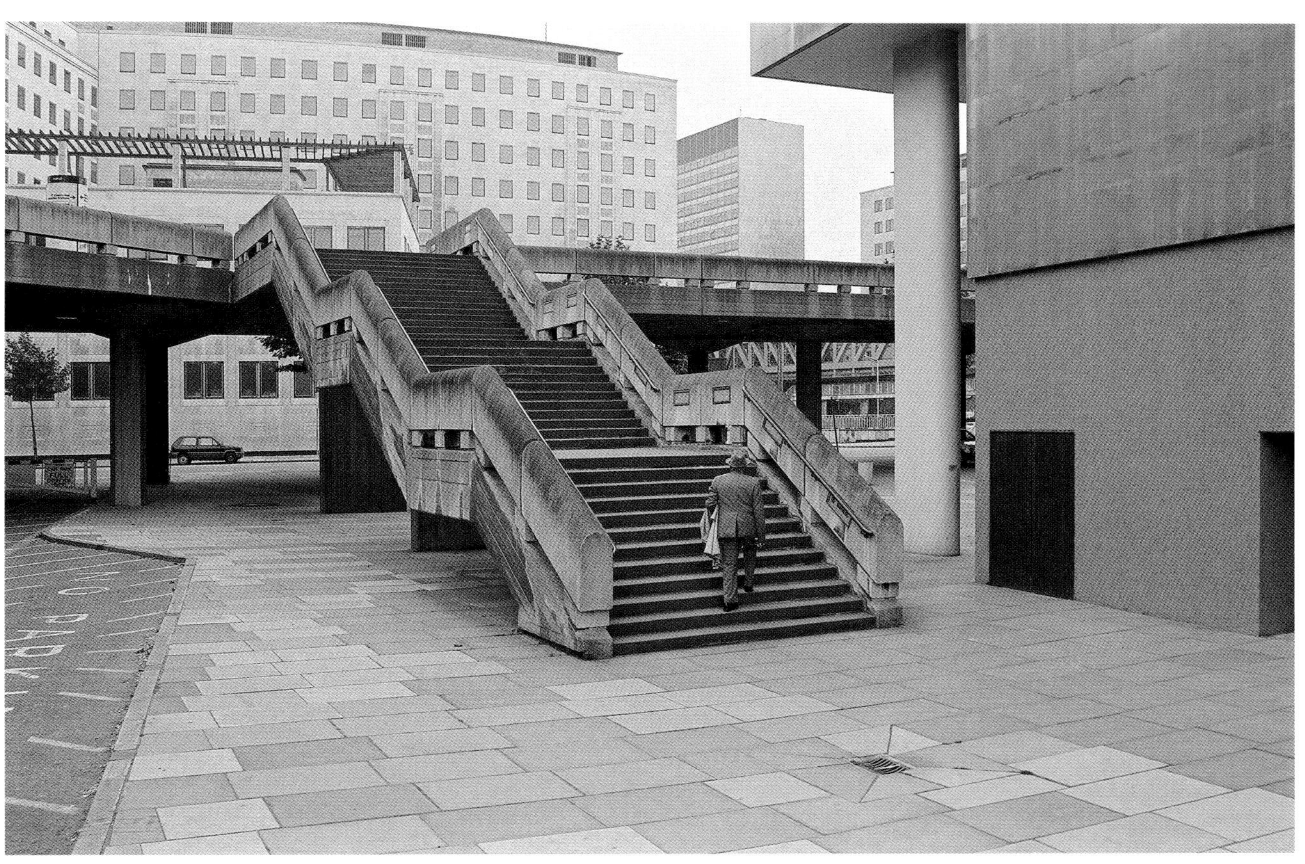

South Bank SE1, 1980

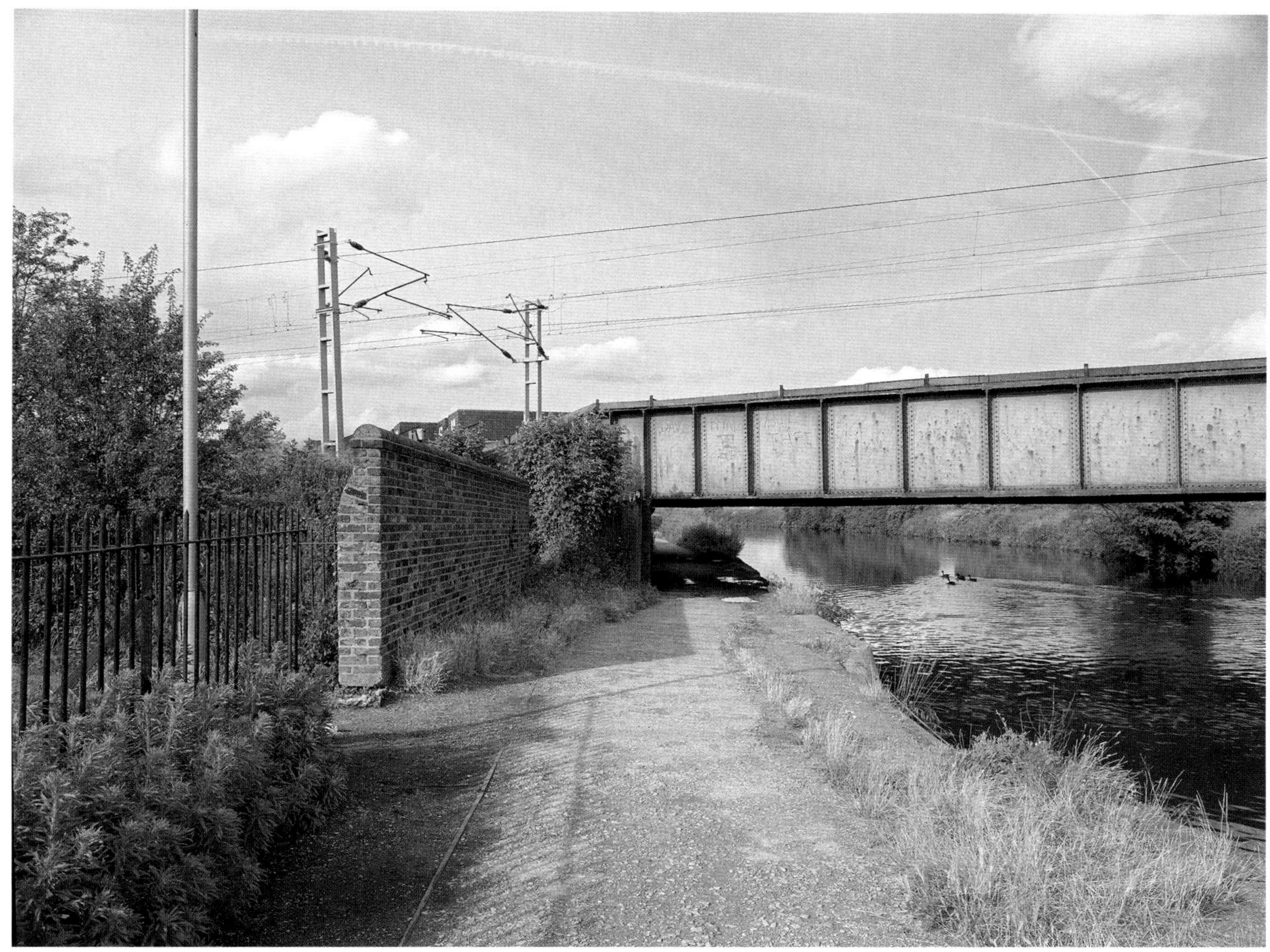

River Lea N15, 1985

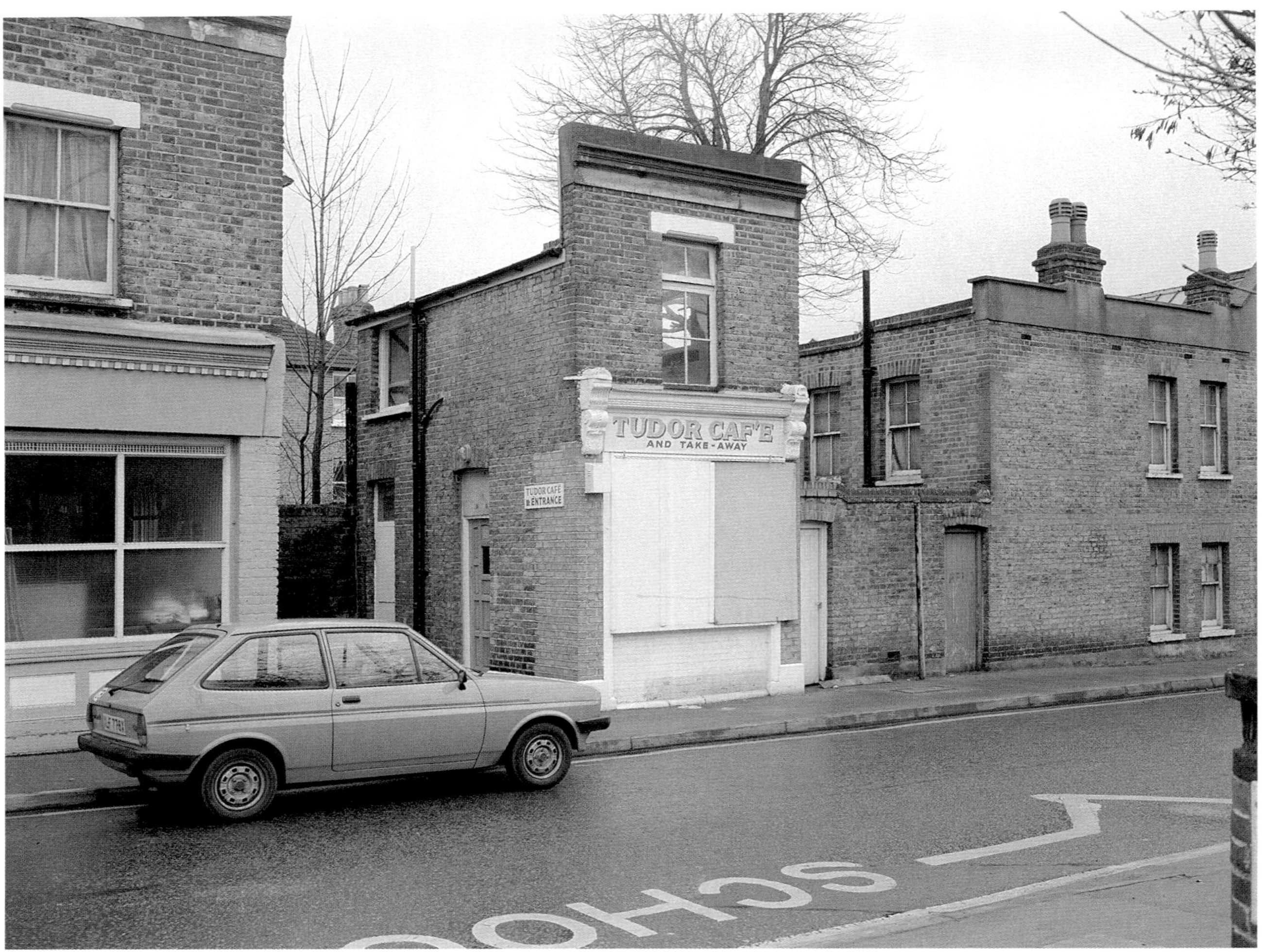

Oldhill Street N16, 1987

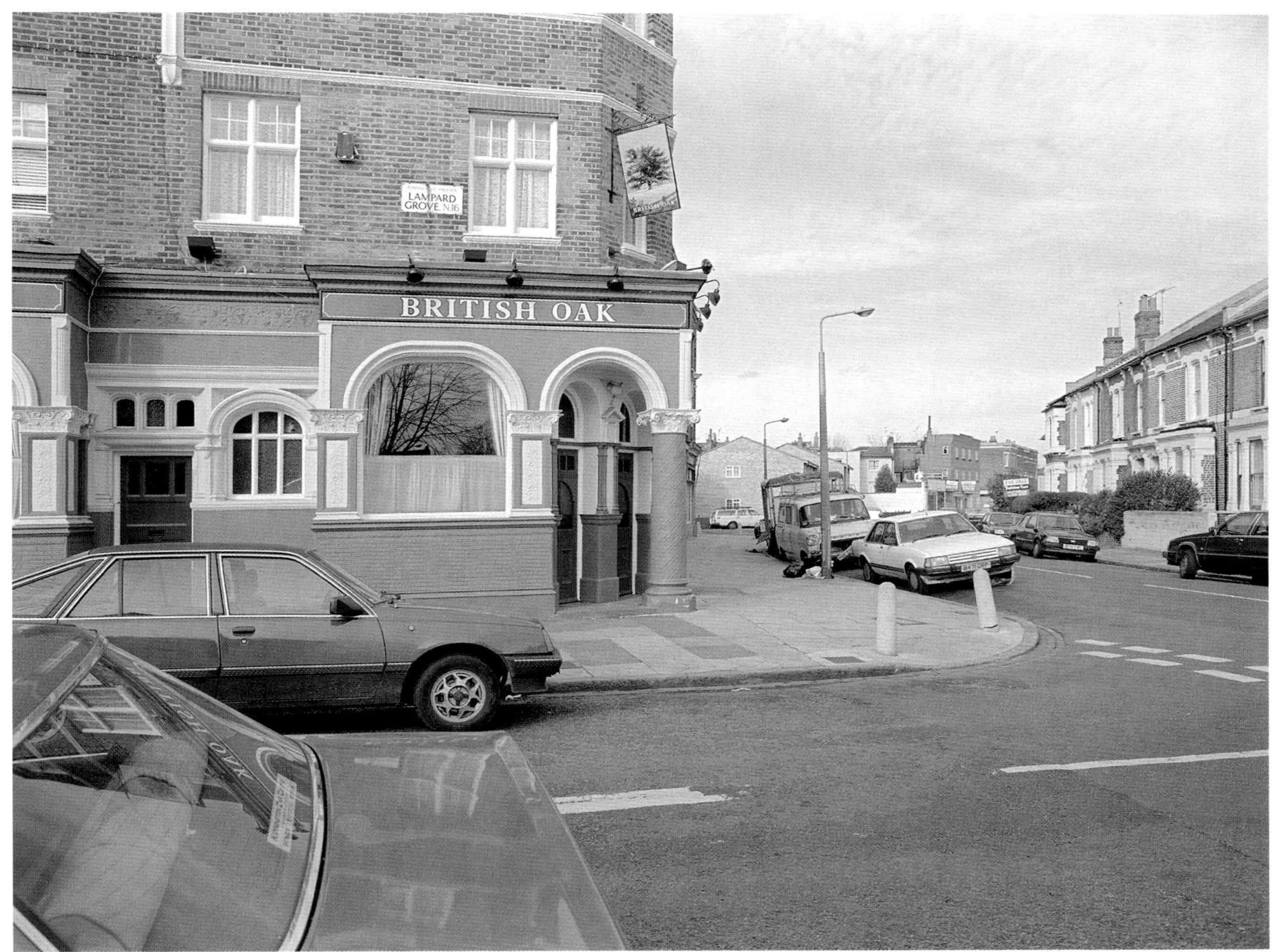

Lampard Grove N16, 1988

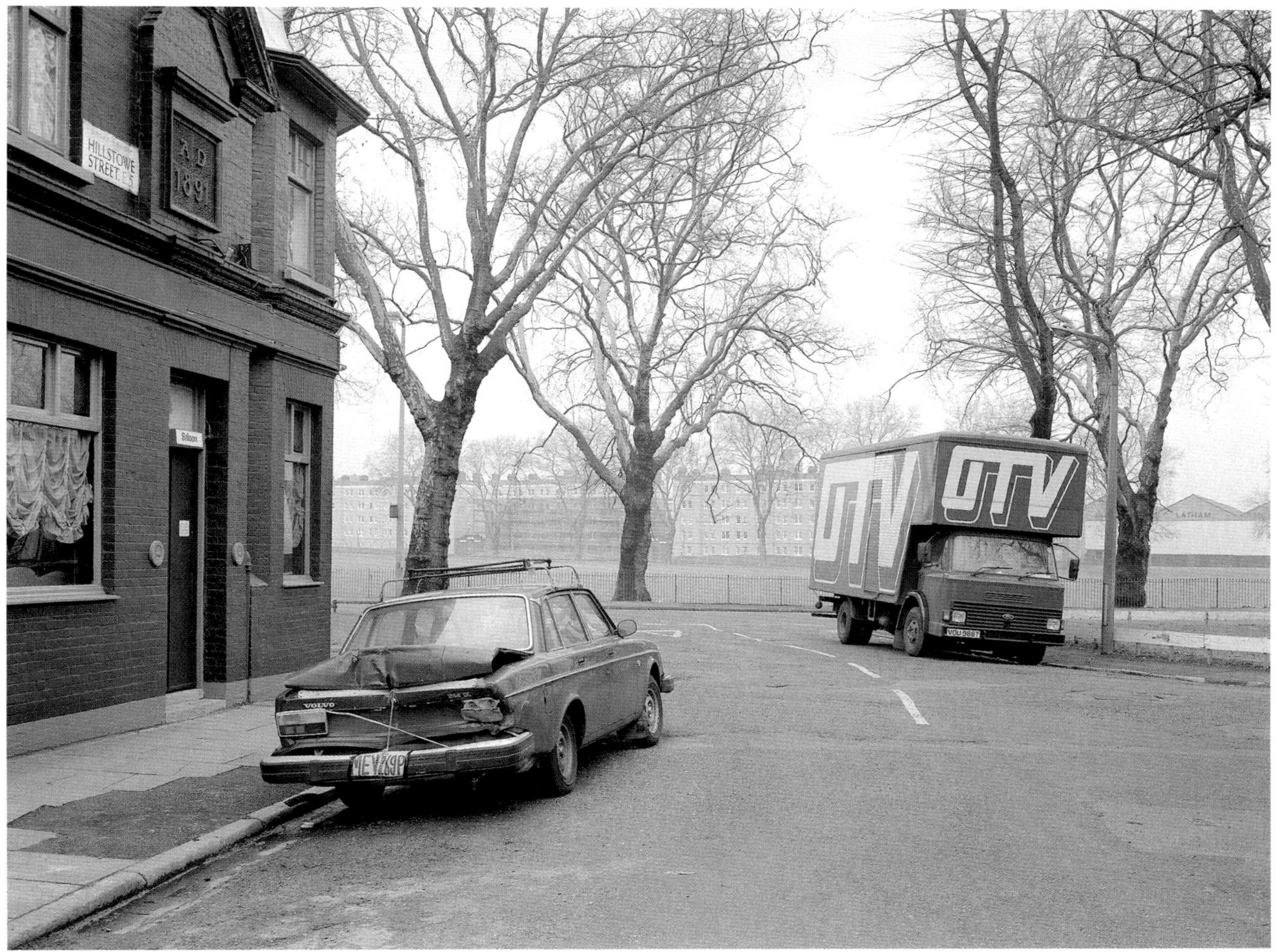

Hillstowe Street E5, 1986

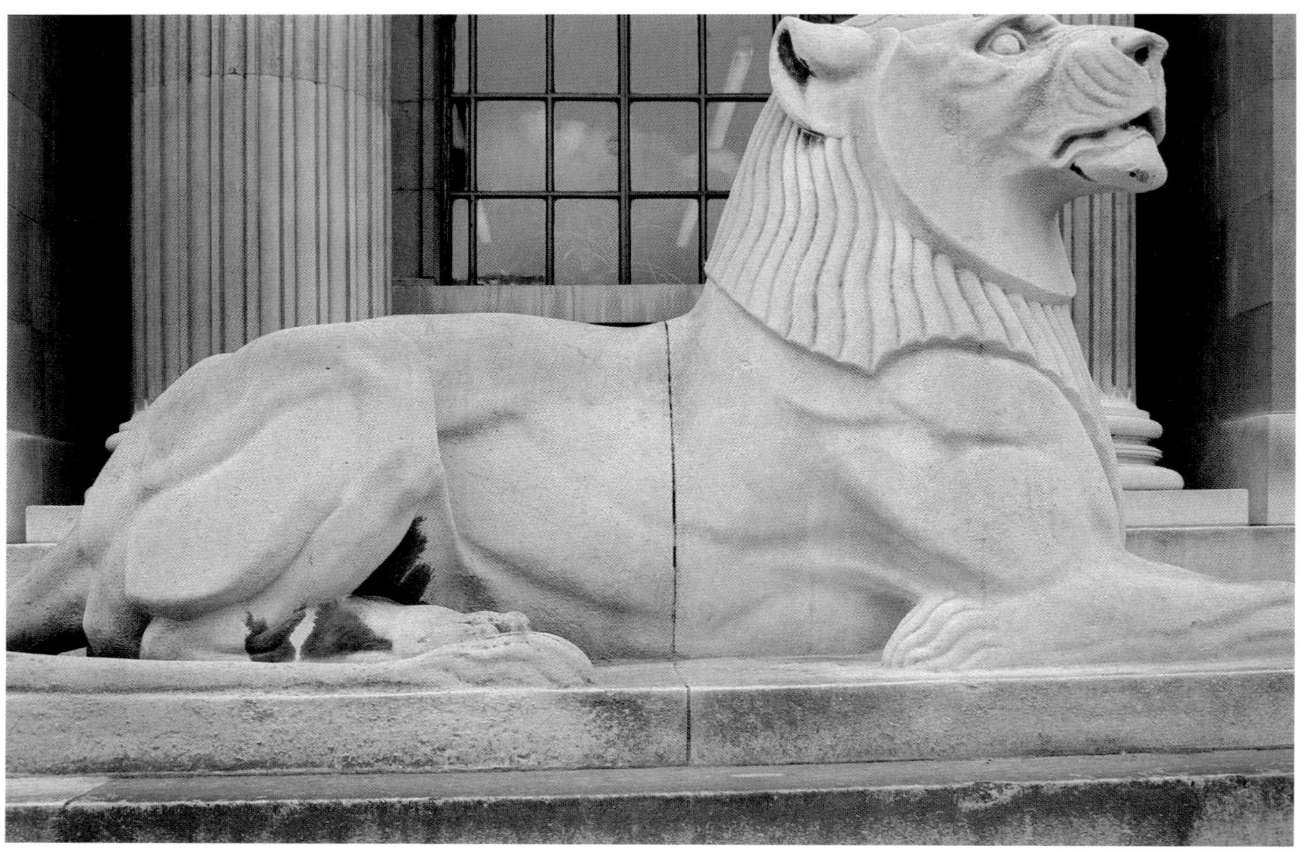

Old Marylebone Town Hall NW1, 1983

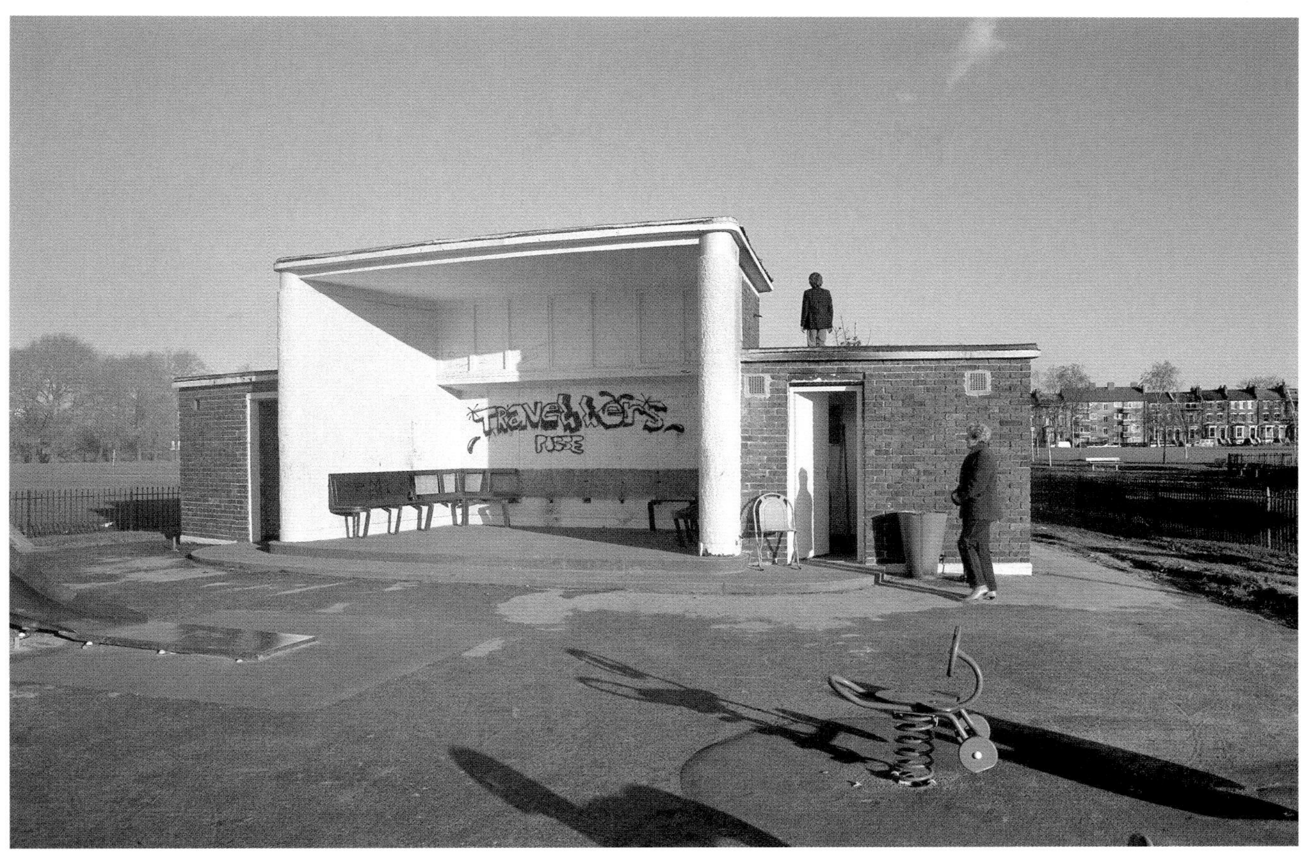

Hackney Downs E5, 1985

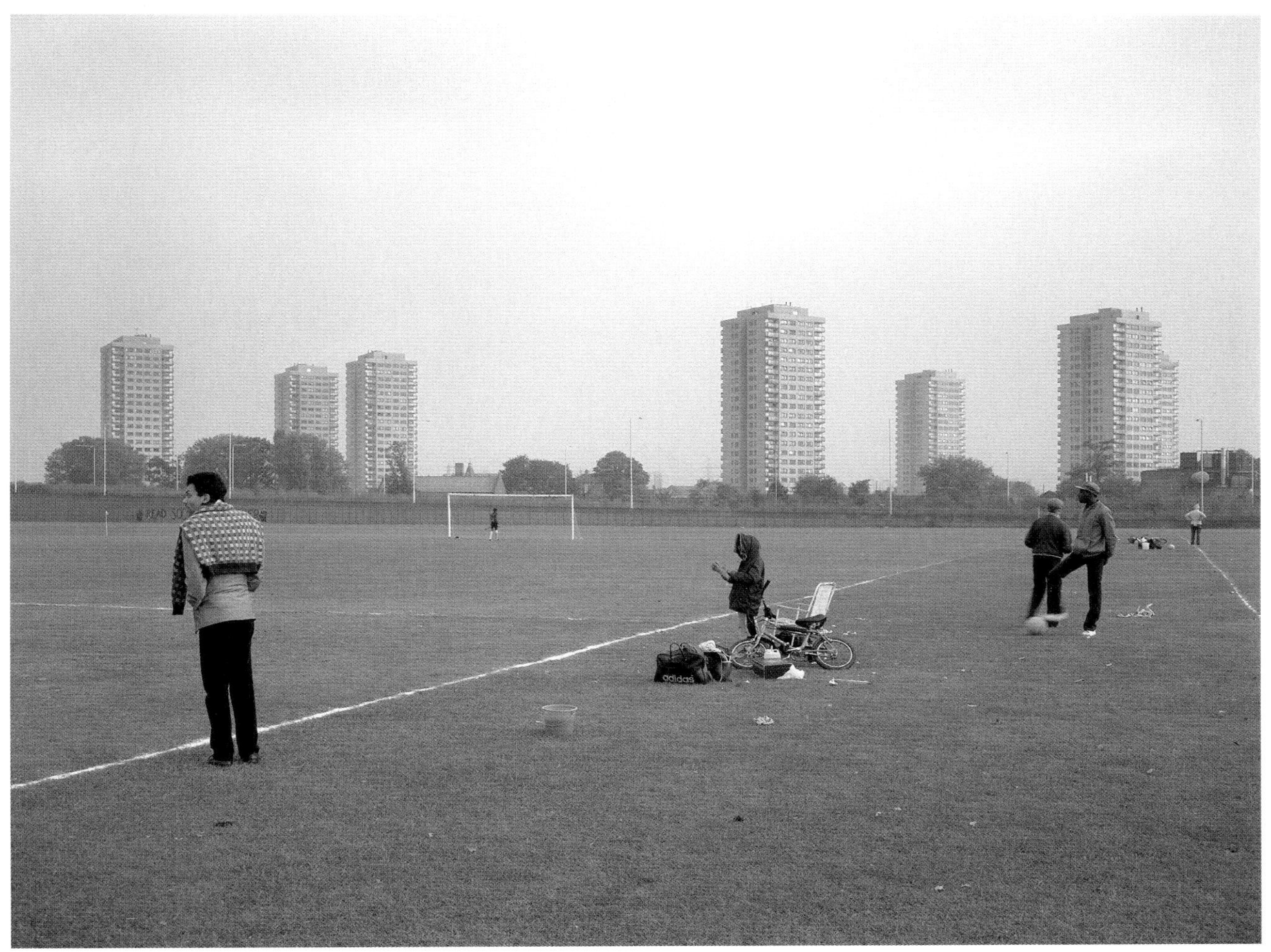

Mabley Green and Trowbridge Estate E9, 1985

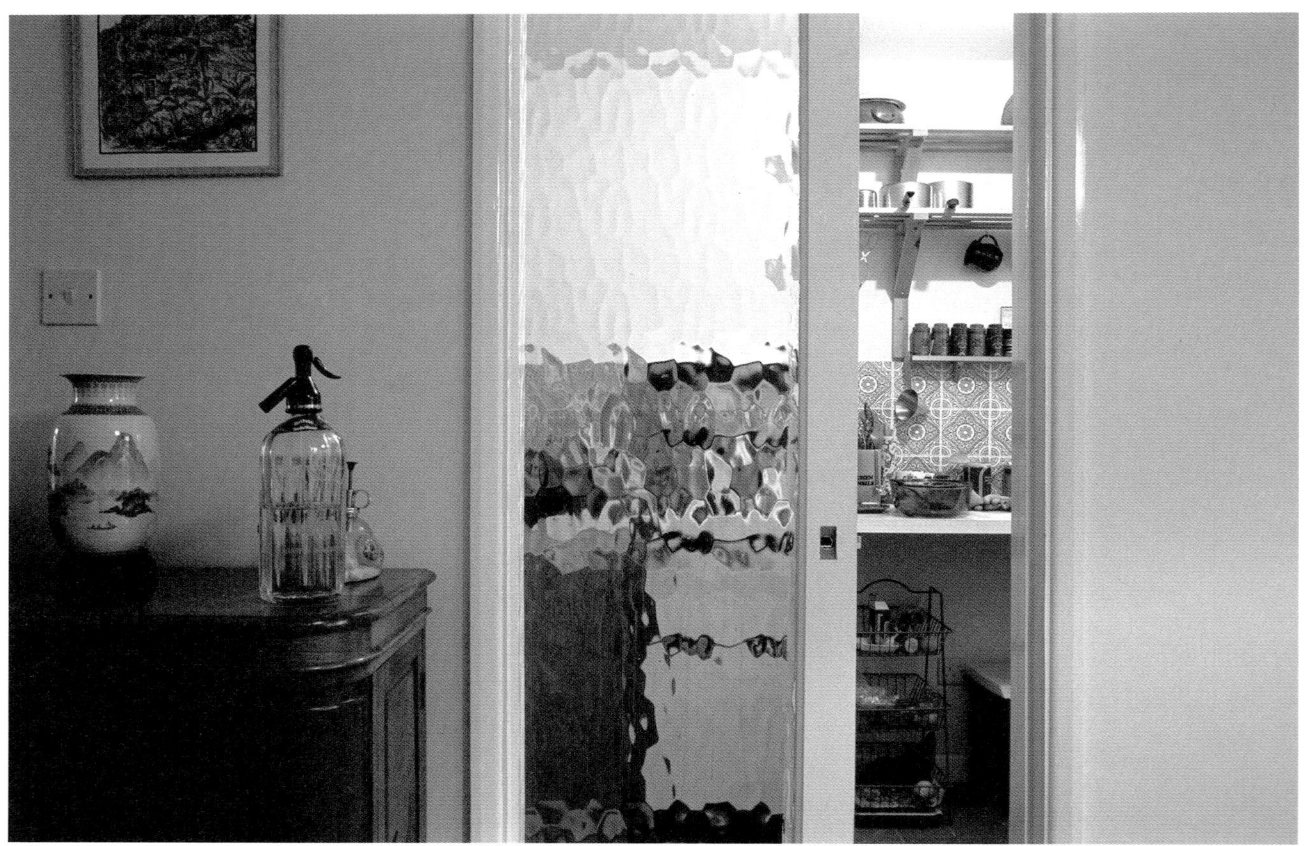

unrecorded location, 1982

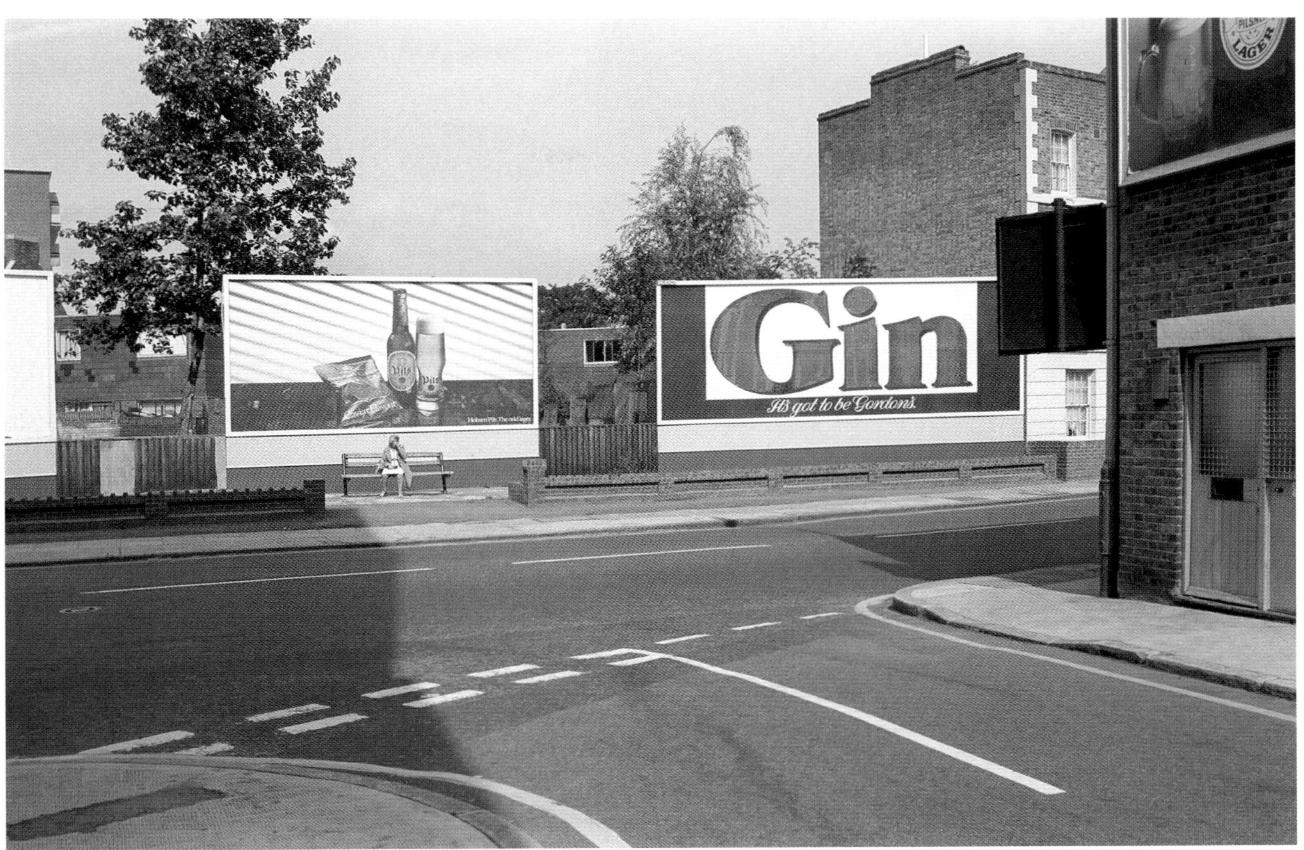

Islington N1, 1983

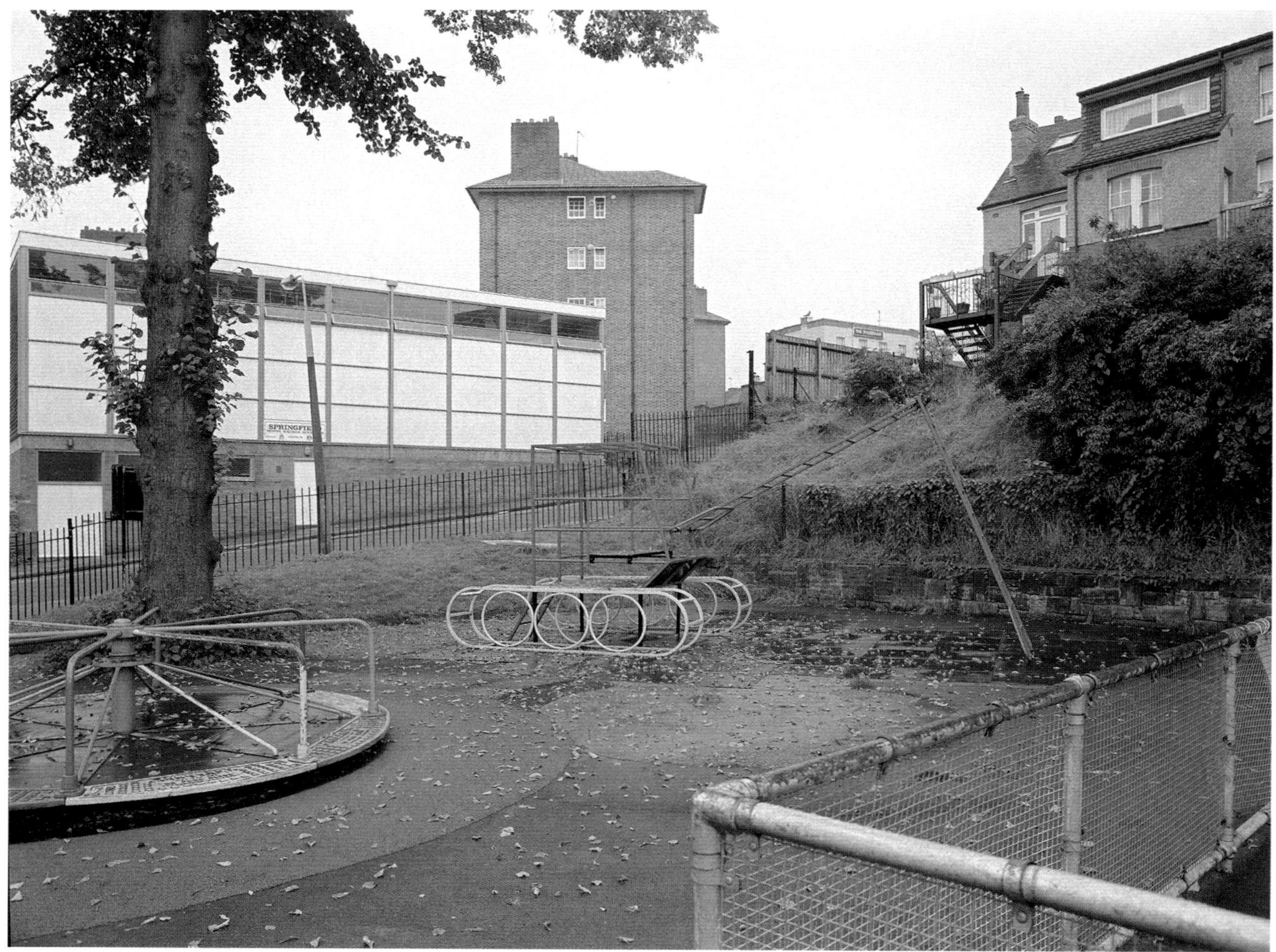

Big Hill E5, 1987

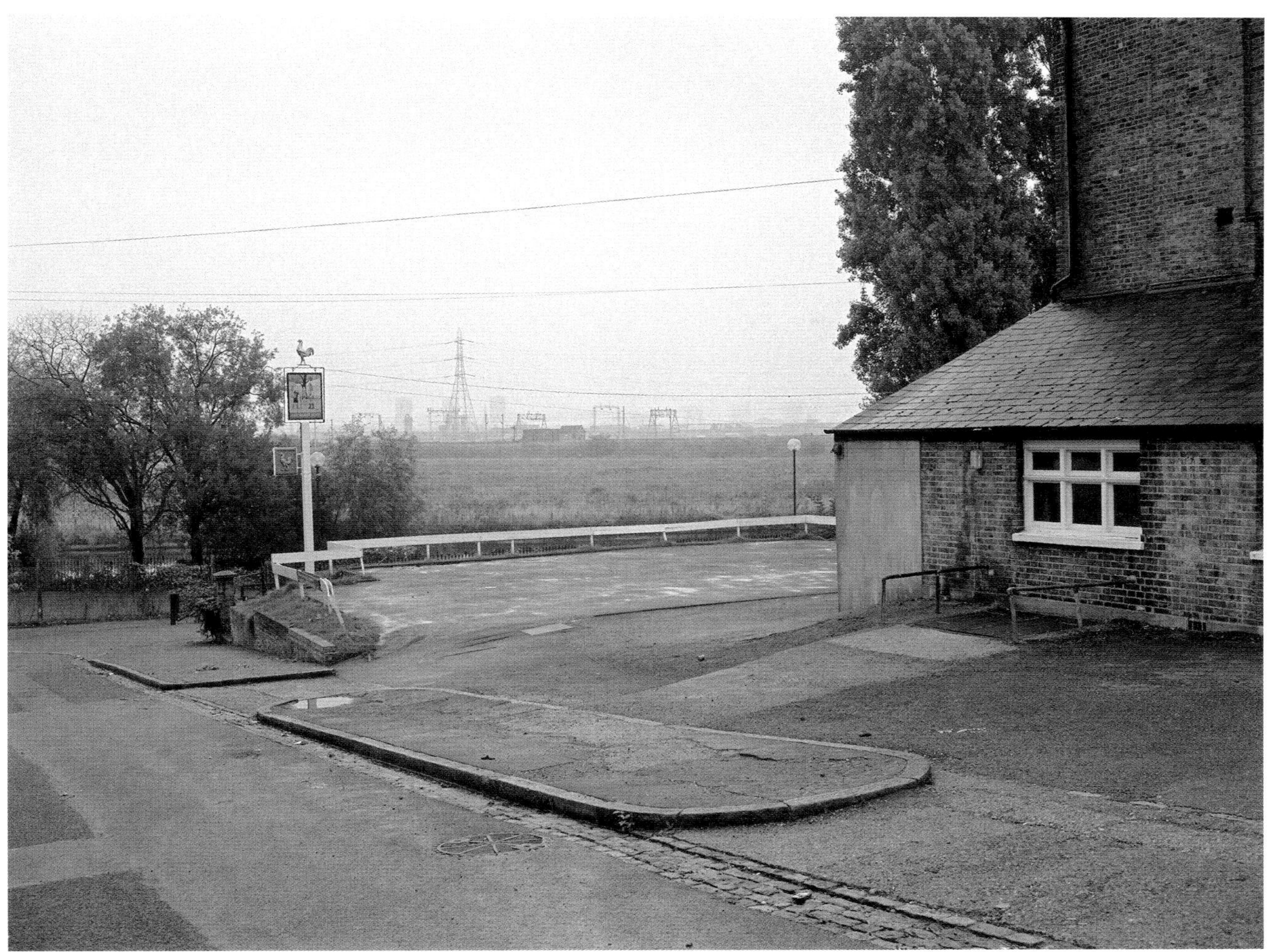

The Robin Hood E5, 1987

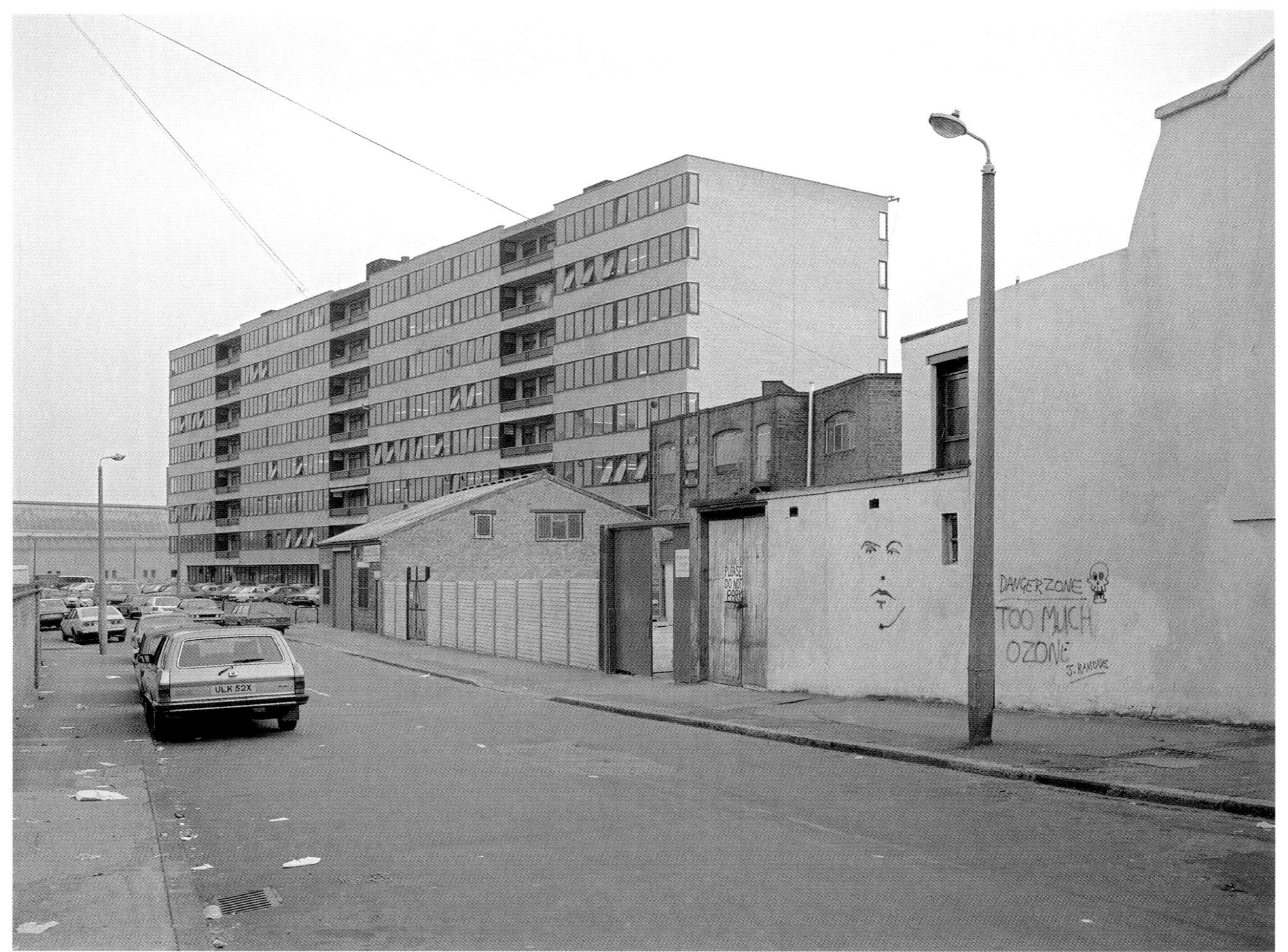

Ada Street E8, 1985

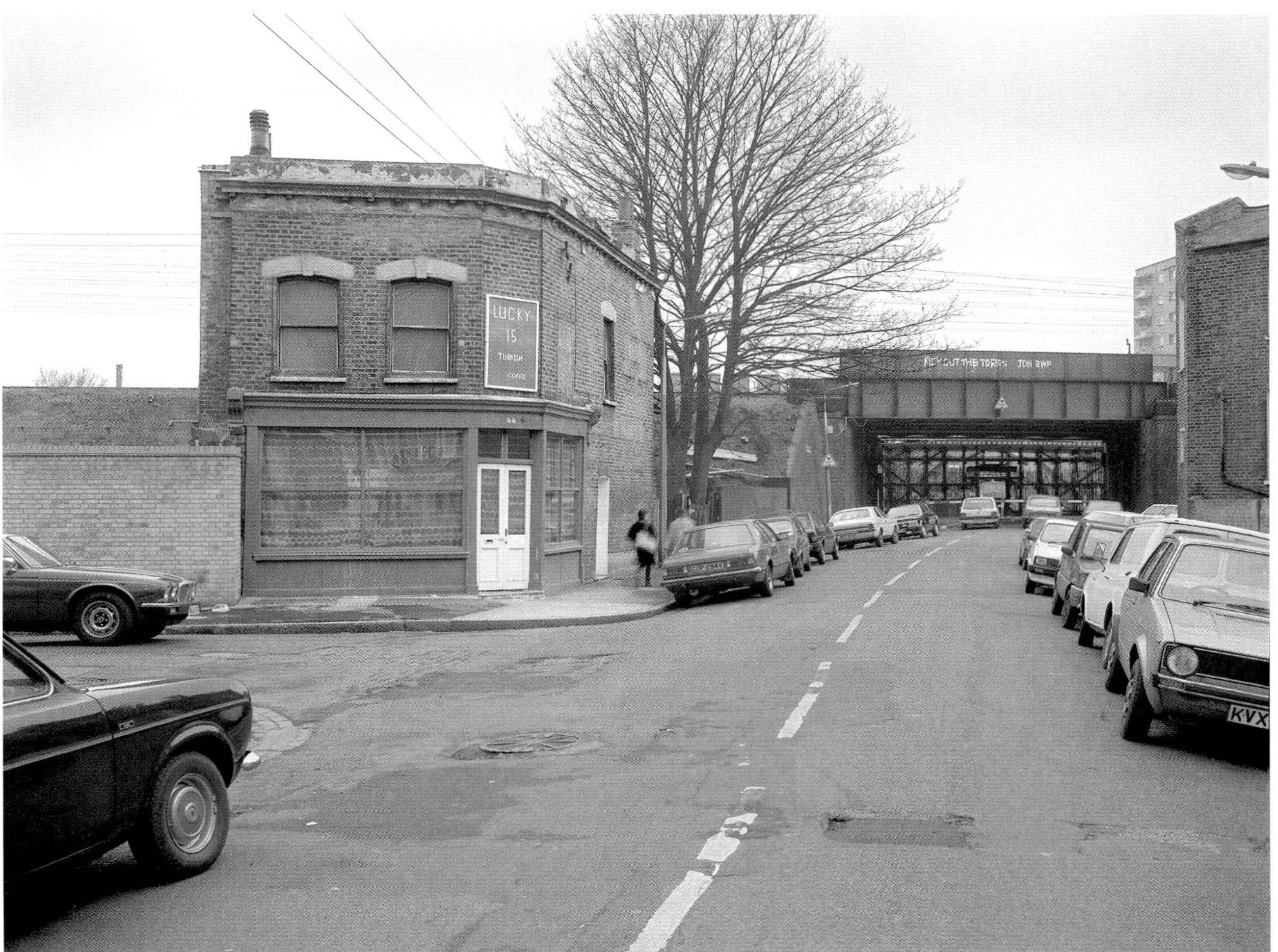

Wilton Way E8, 1986

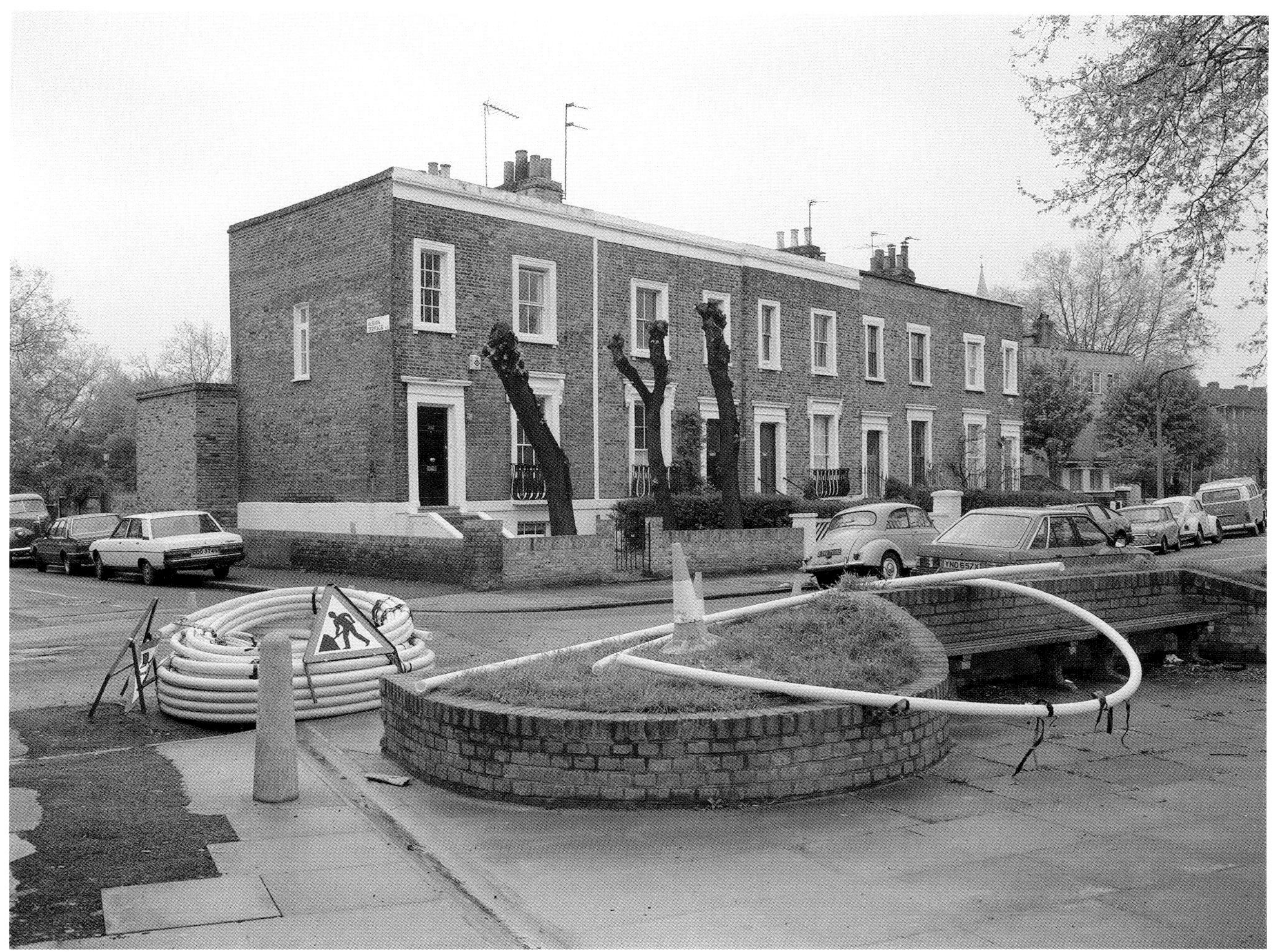

Mayfield Road E8, 1986

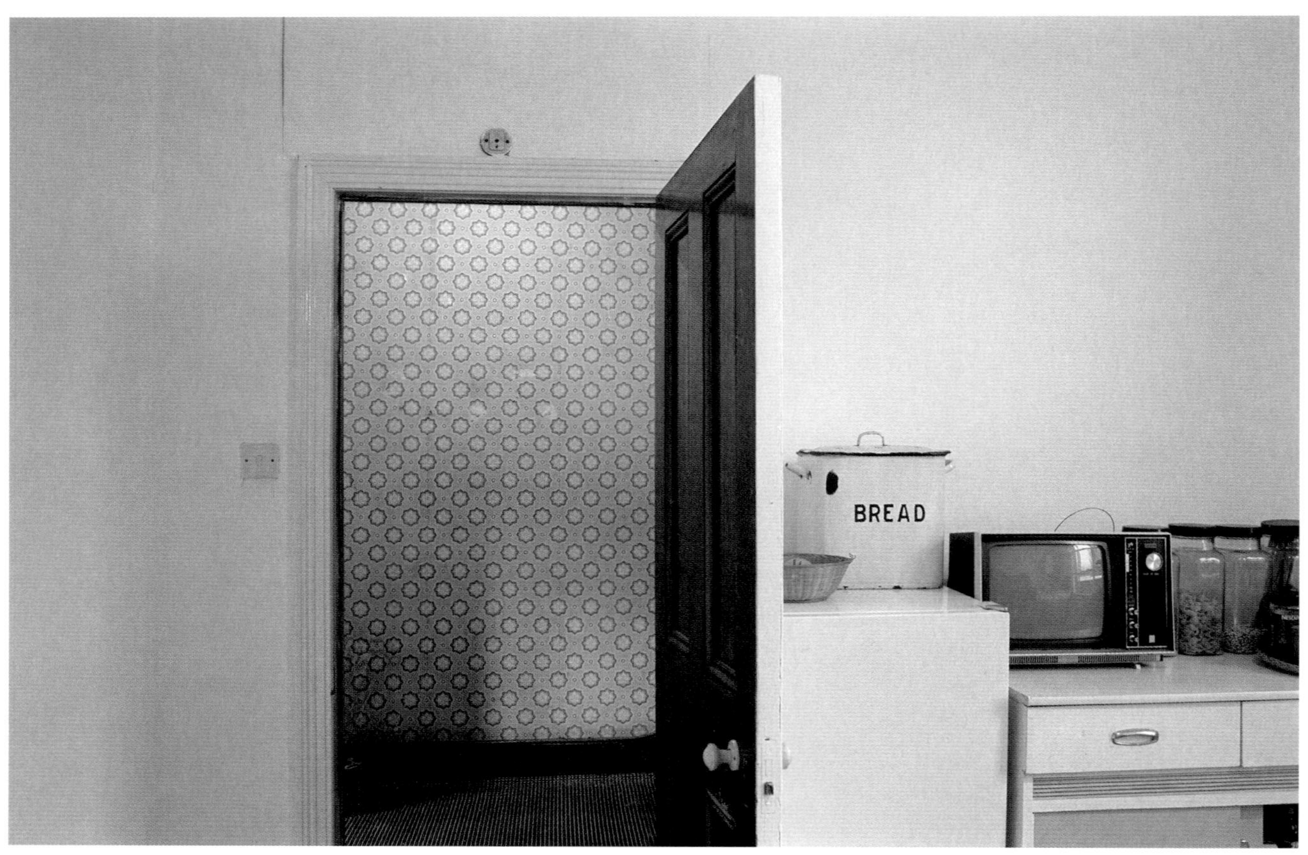

Camden Town NW1, 1982

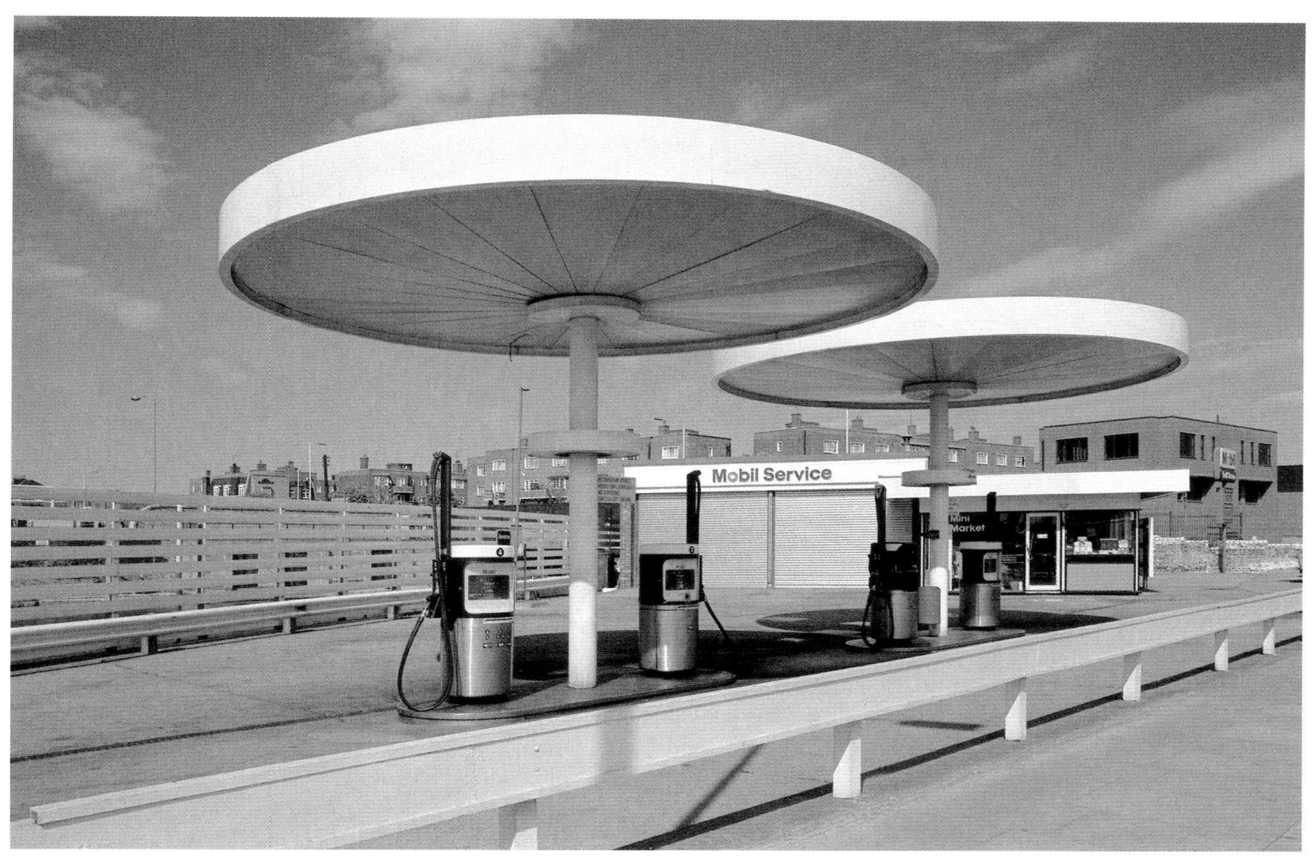

King's Cross N1, 1984

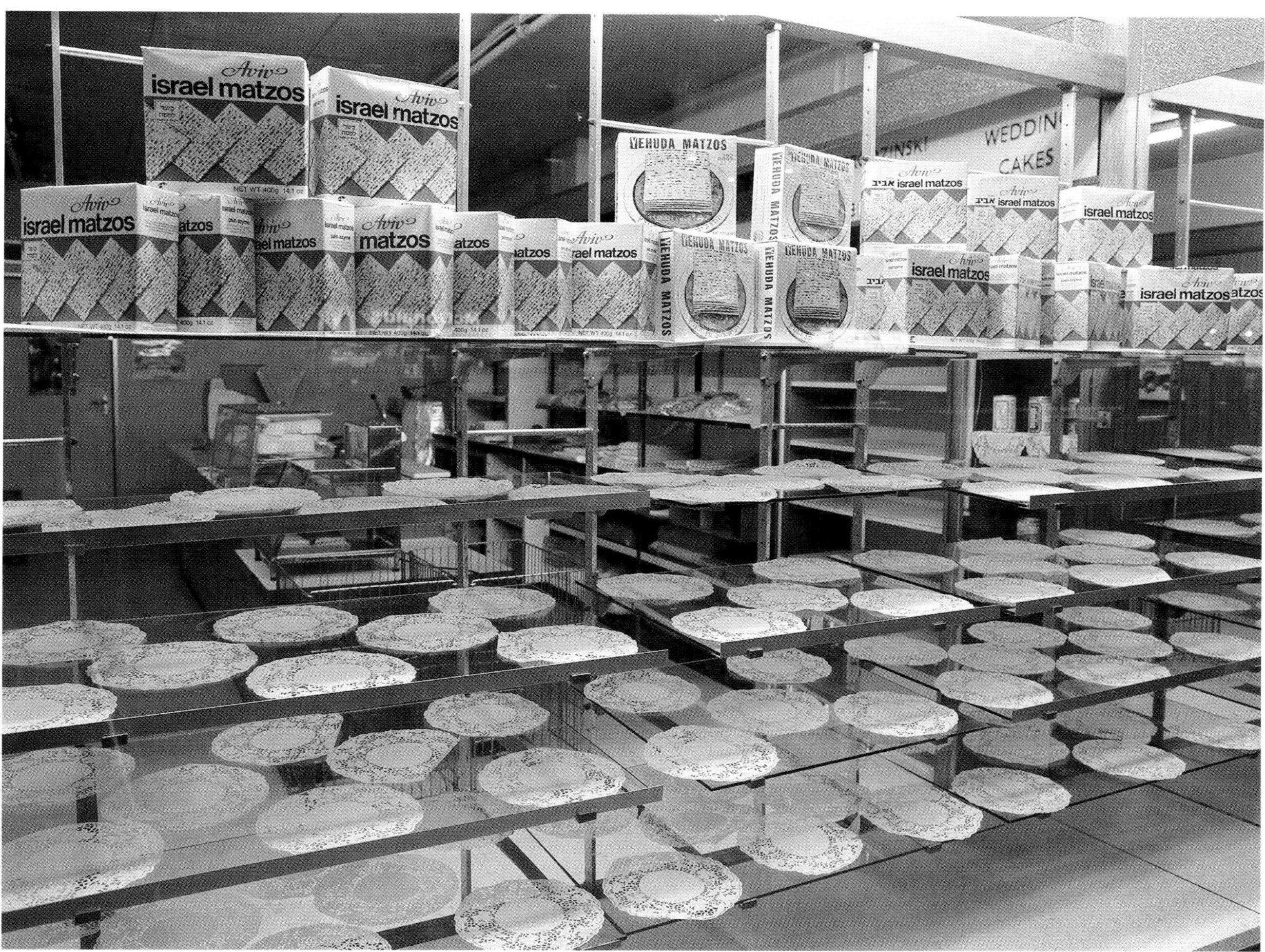

Stamford Hill N16, 1985

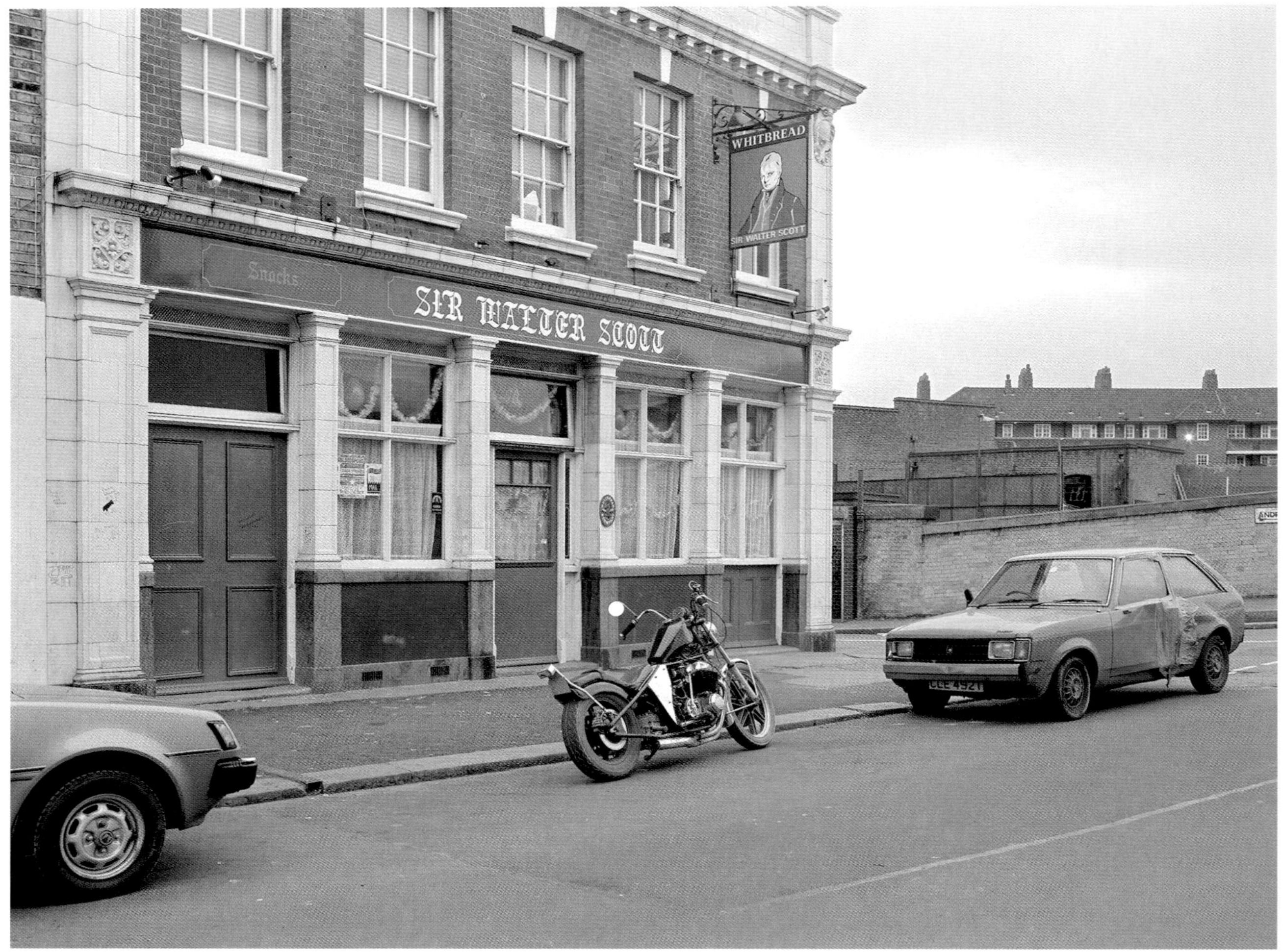

Broadway Market E8, 1985

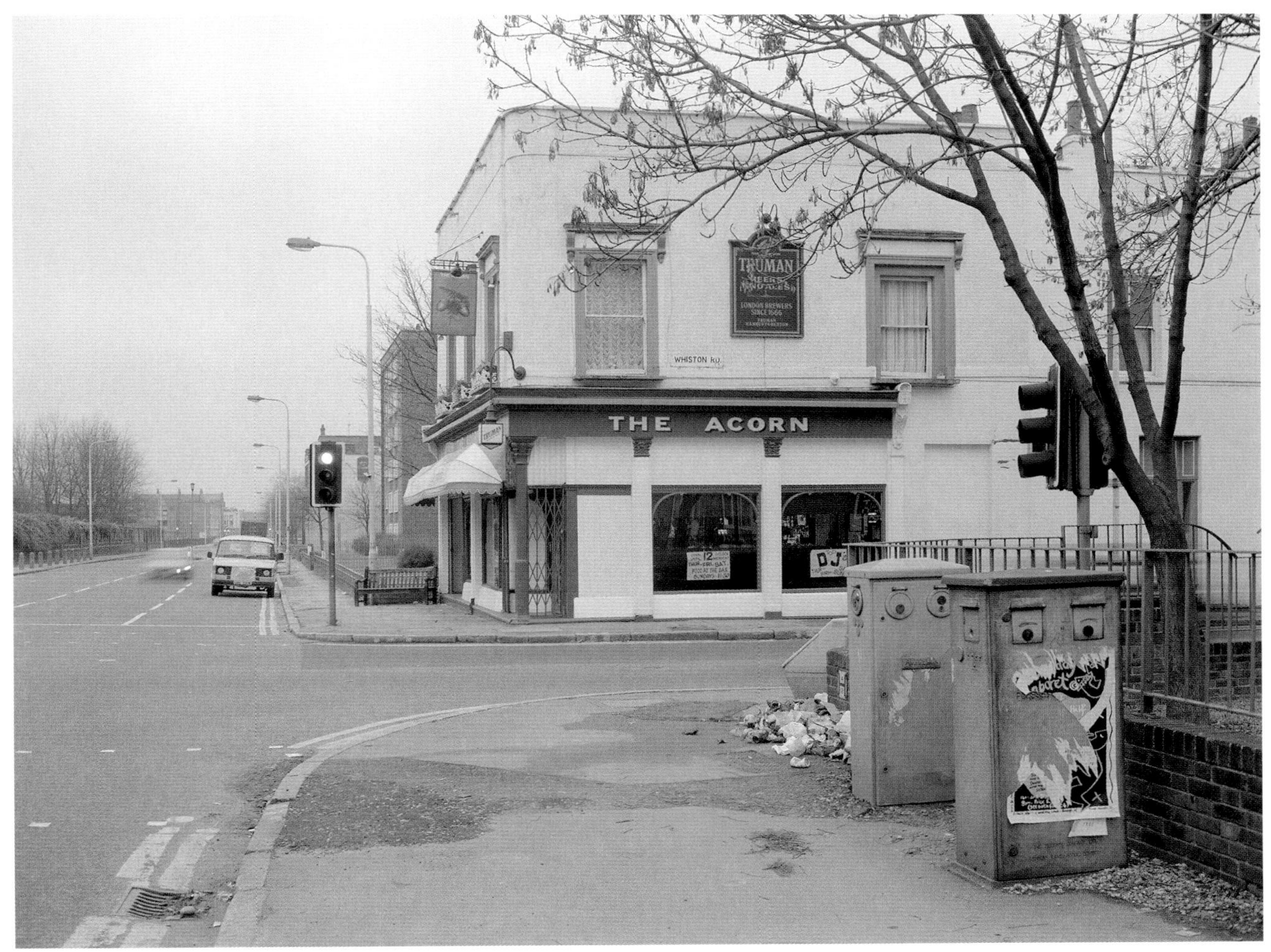

Queensbridge Road E2, 1985

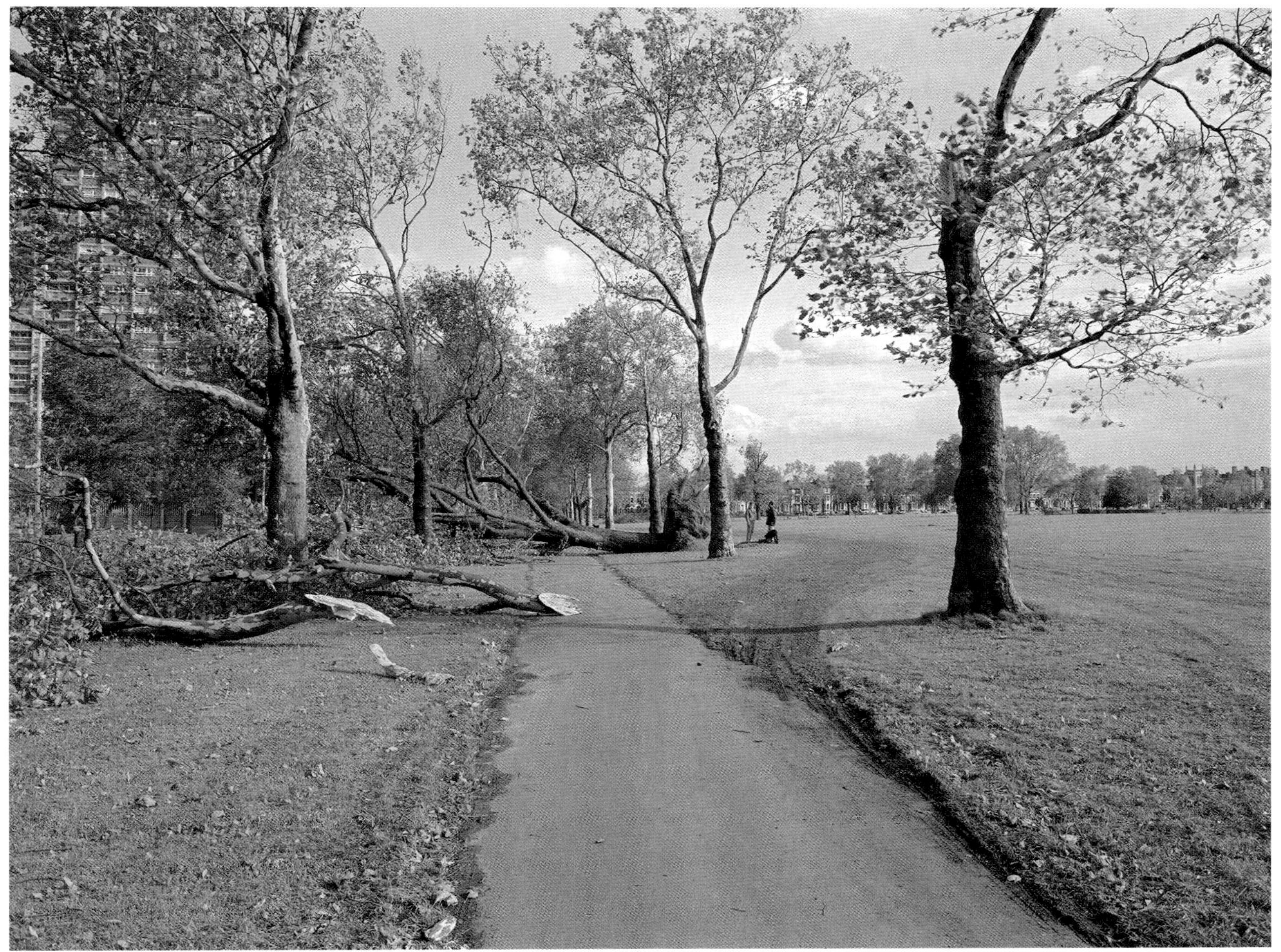

Hackney Downs E5, 1987

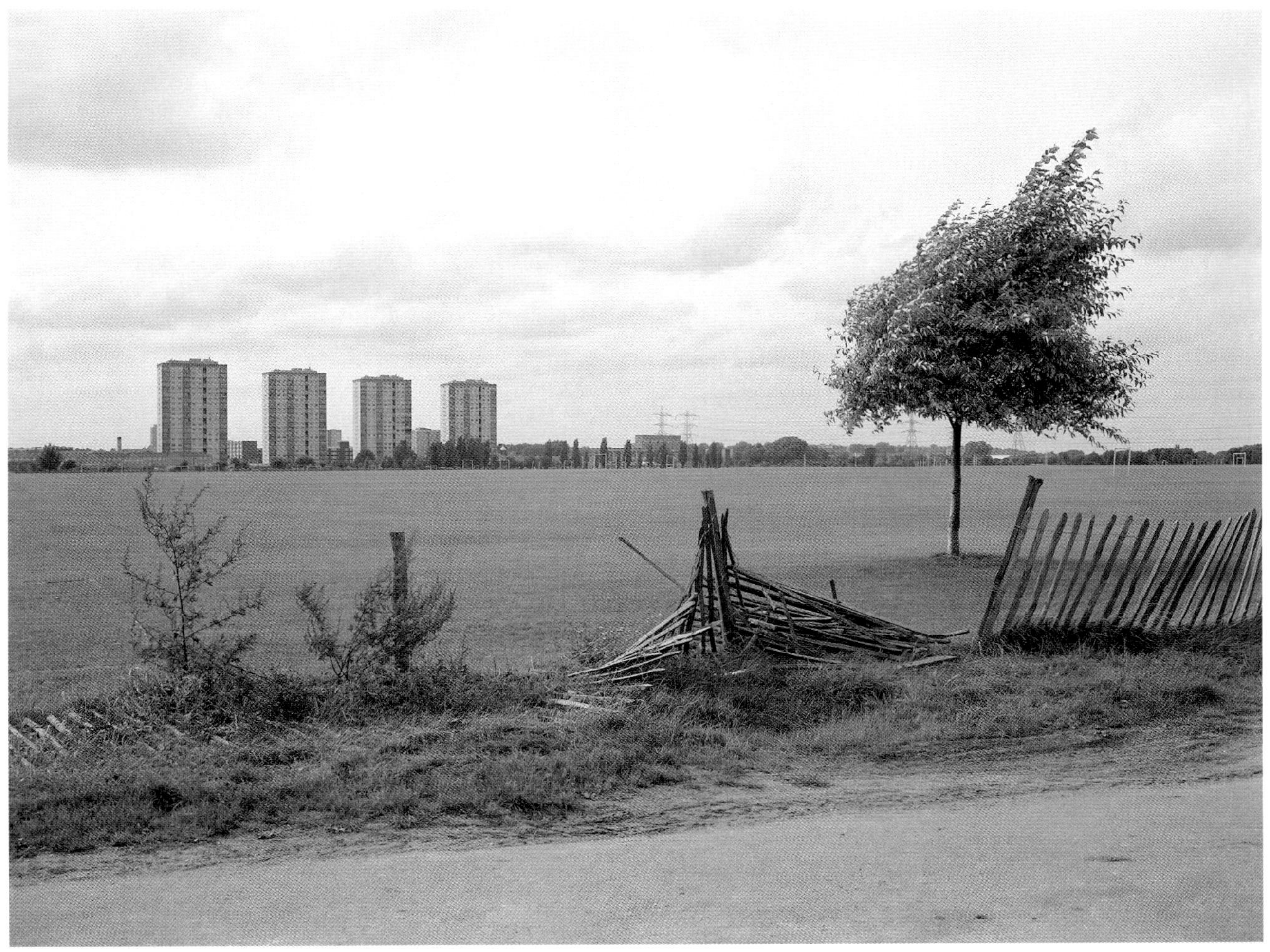

Hackney Marshes E9, 1987

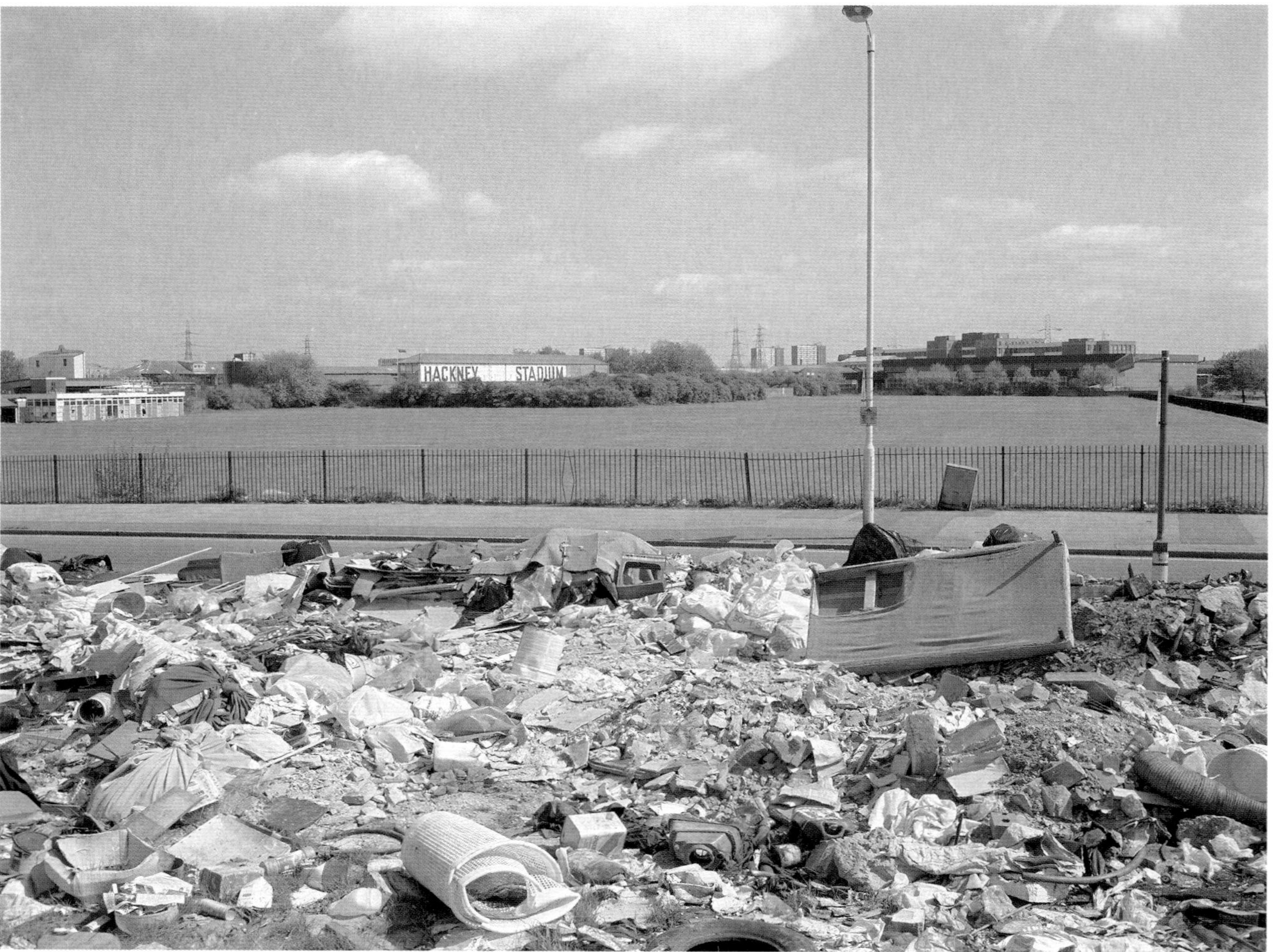

Eastway E9, 1987

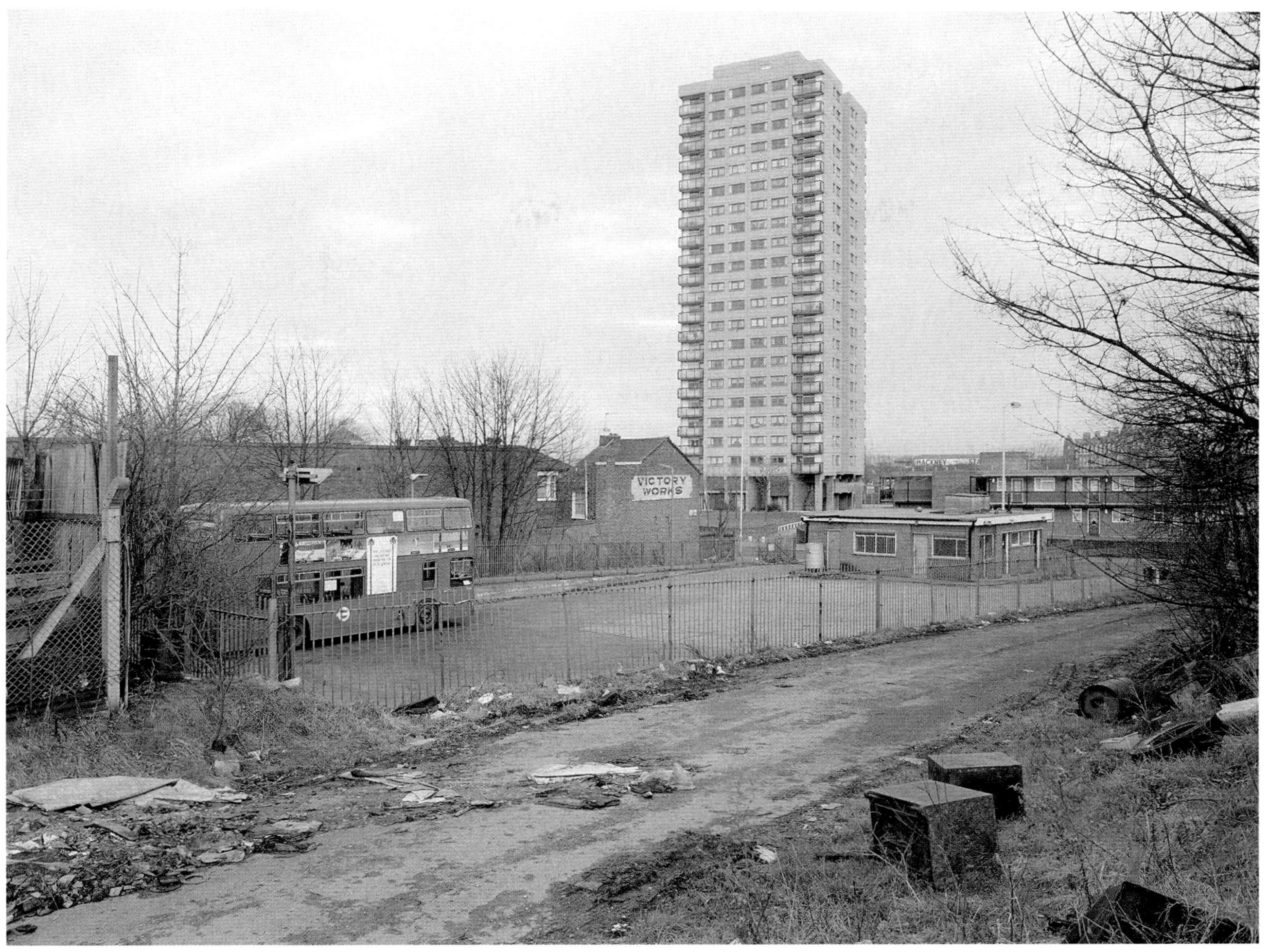

Hackney Wick E9, 1988

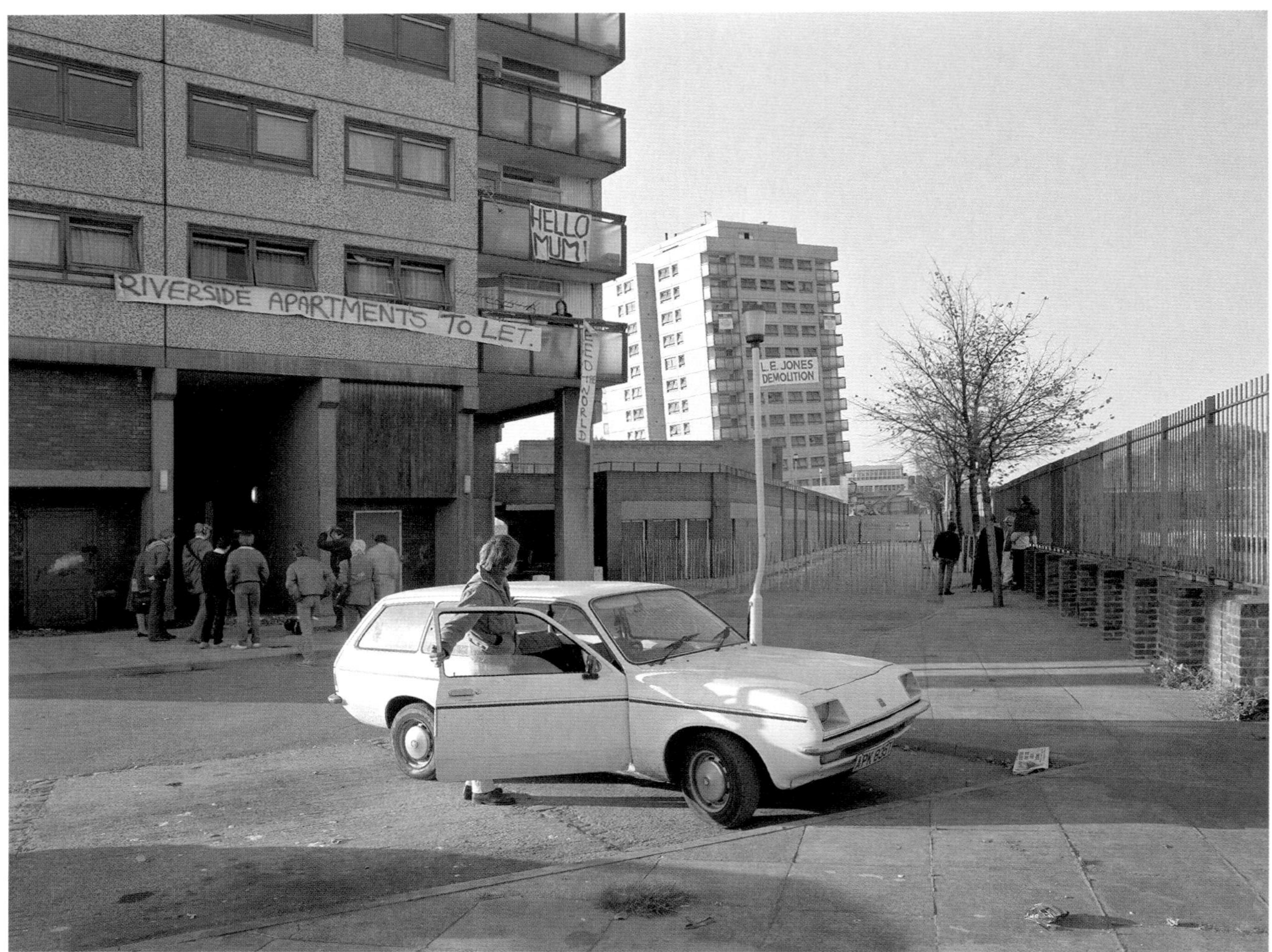

Trowbridge Estate E9, 1985

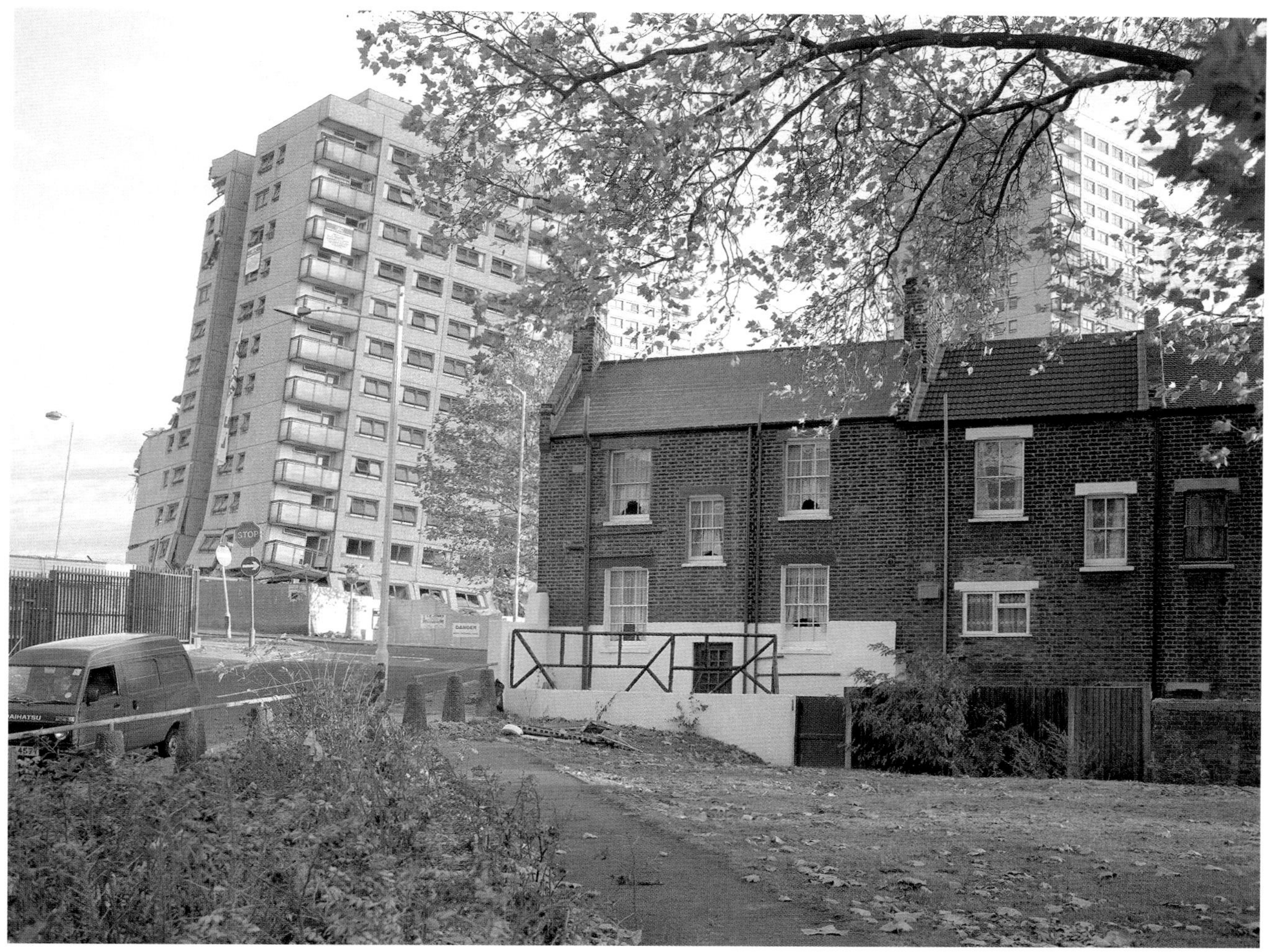

Lee Conservancy Road E9, 1985

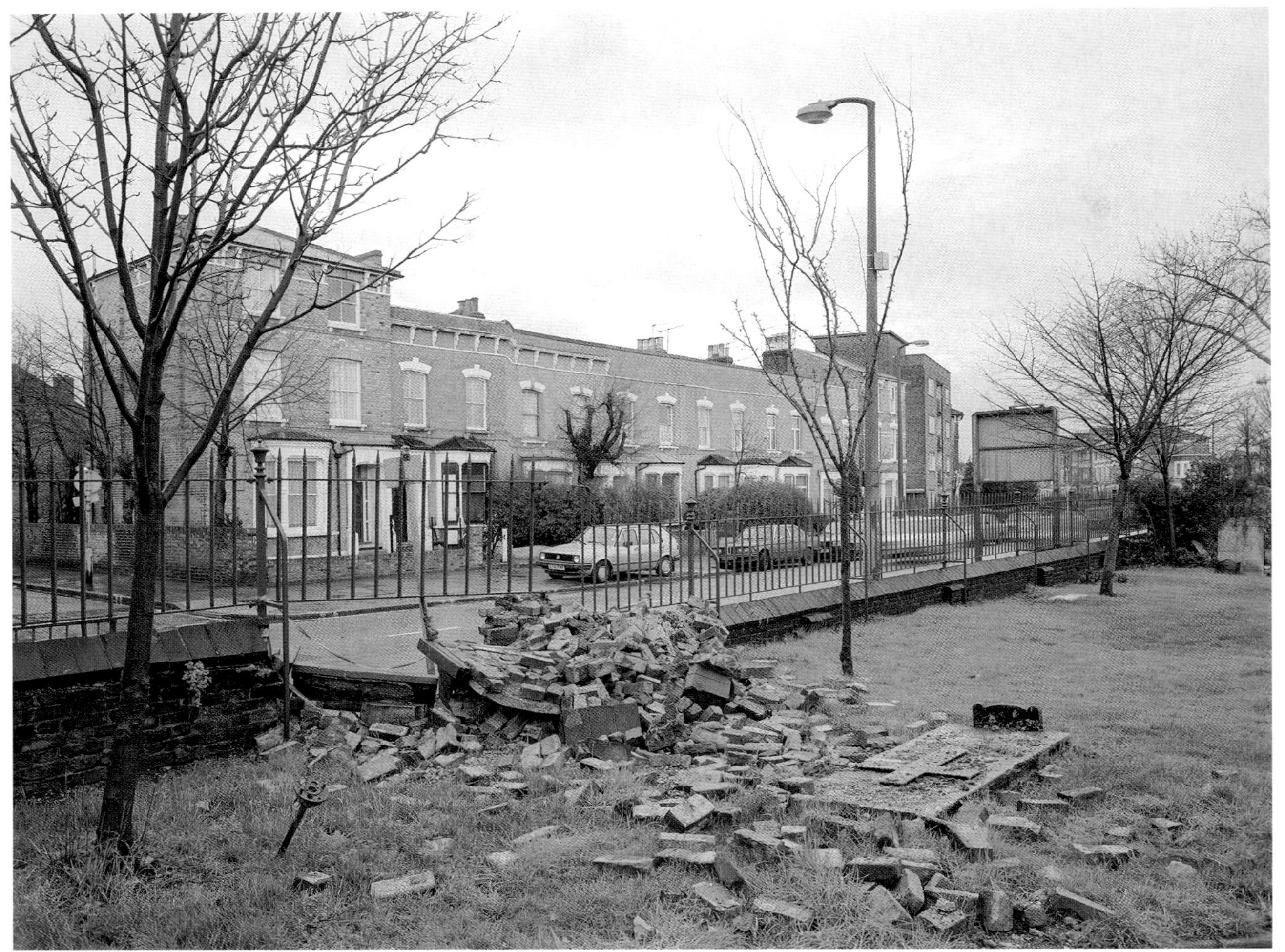

Evering Road N16, 1987

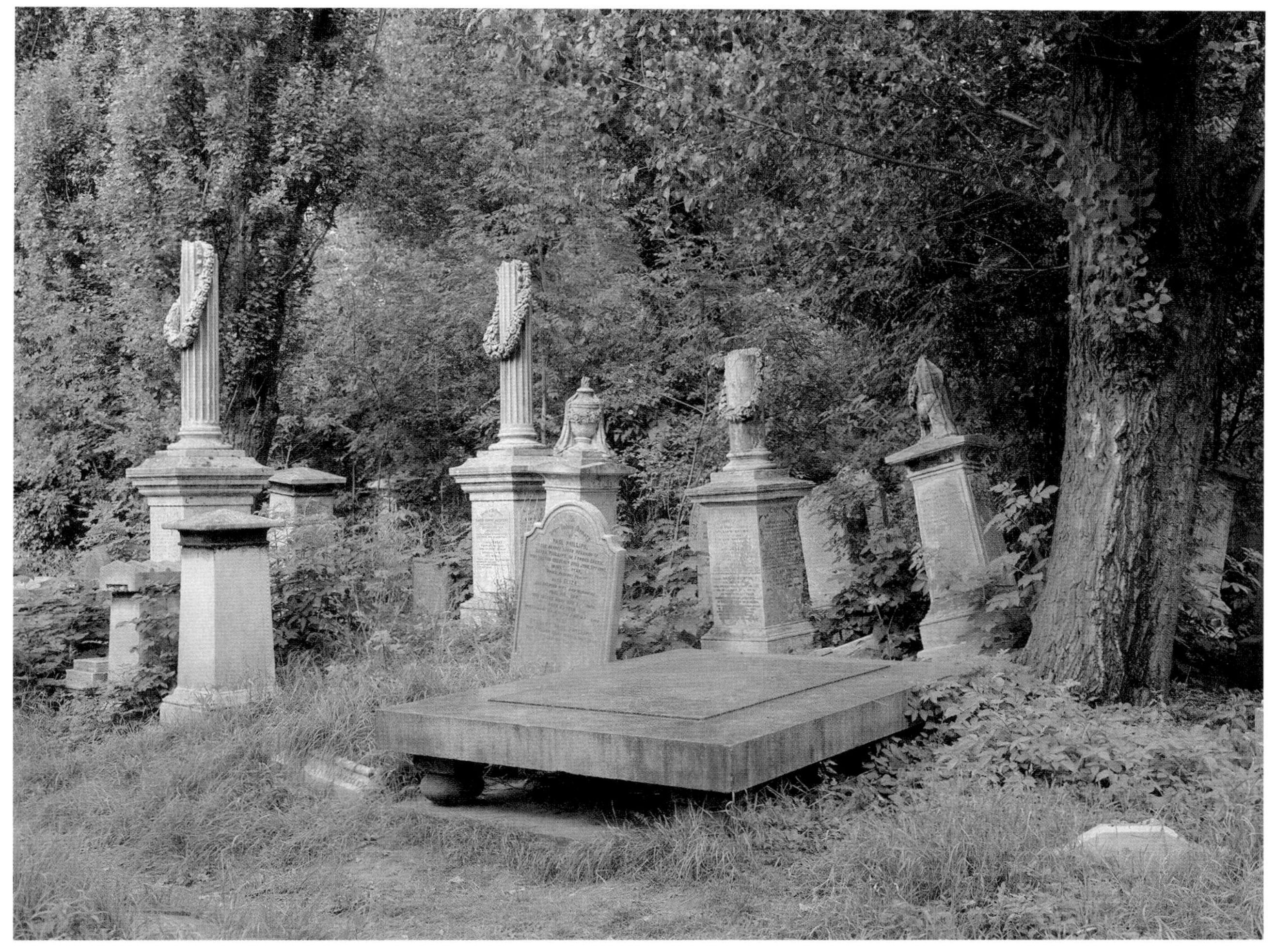

Abney Park Cemetery N16, 1986

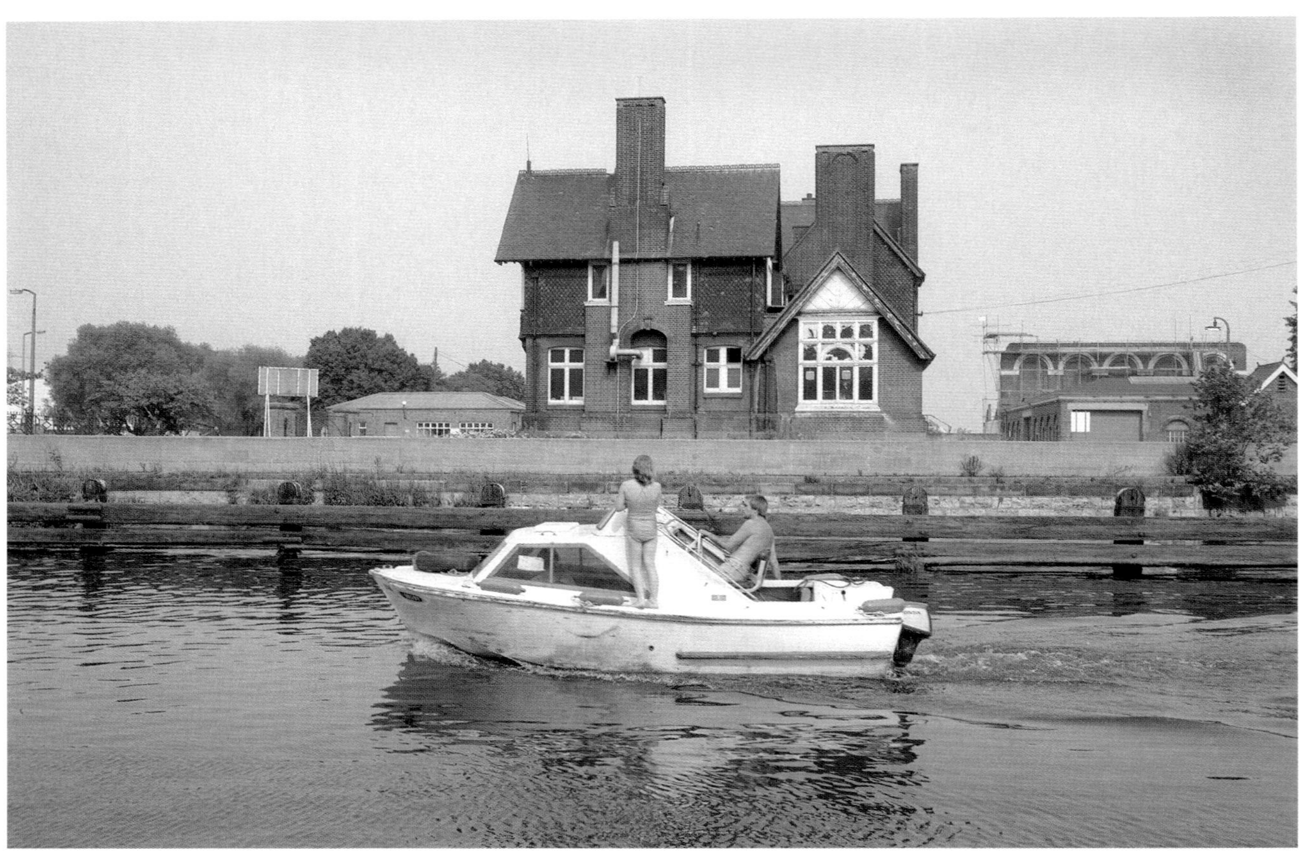

River Lea E5, 1984

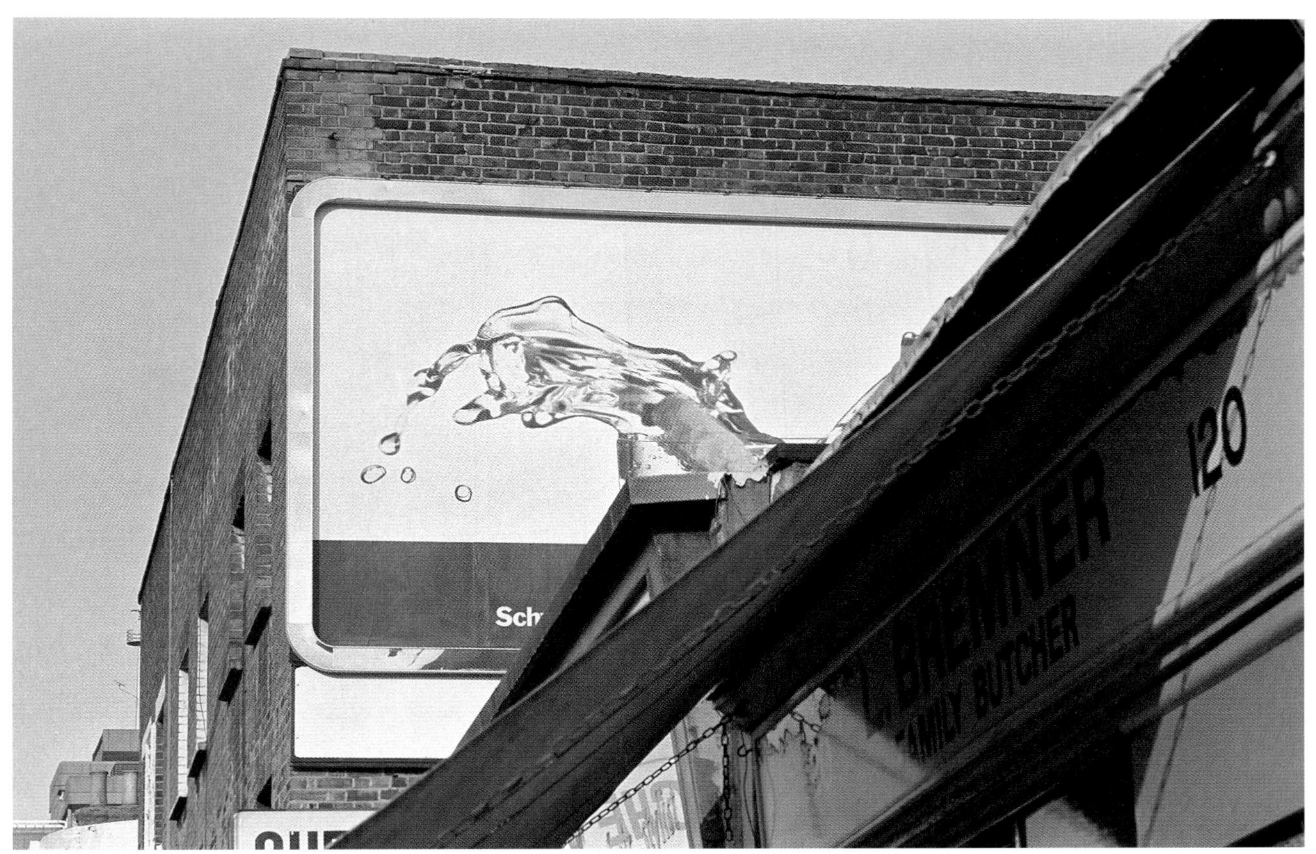

unrecorded location, 1982

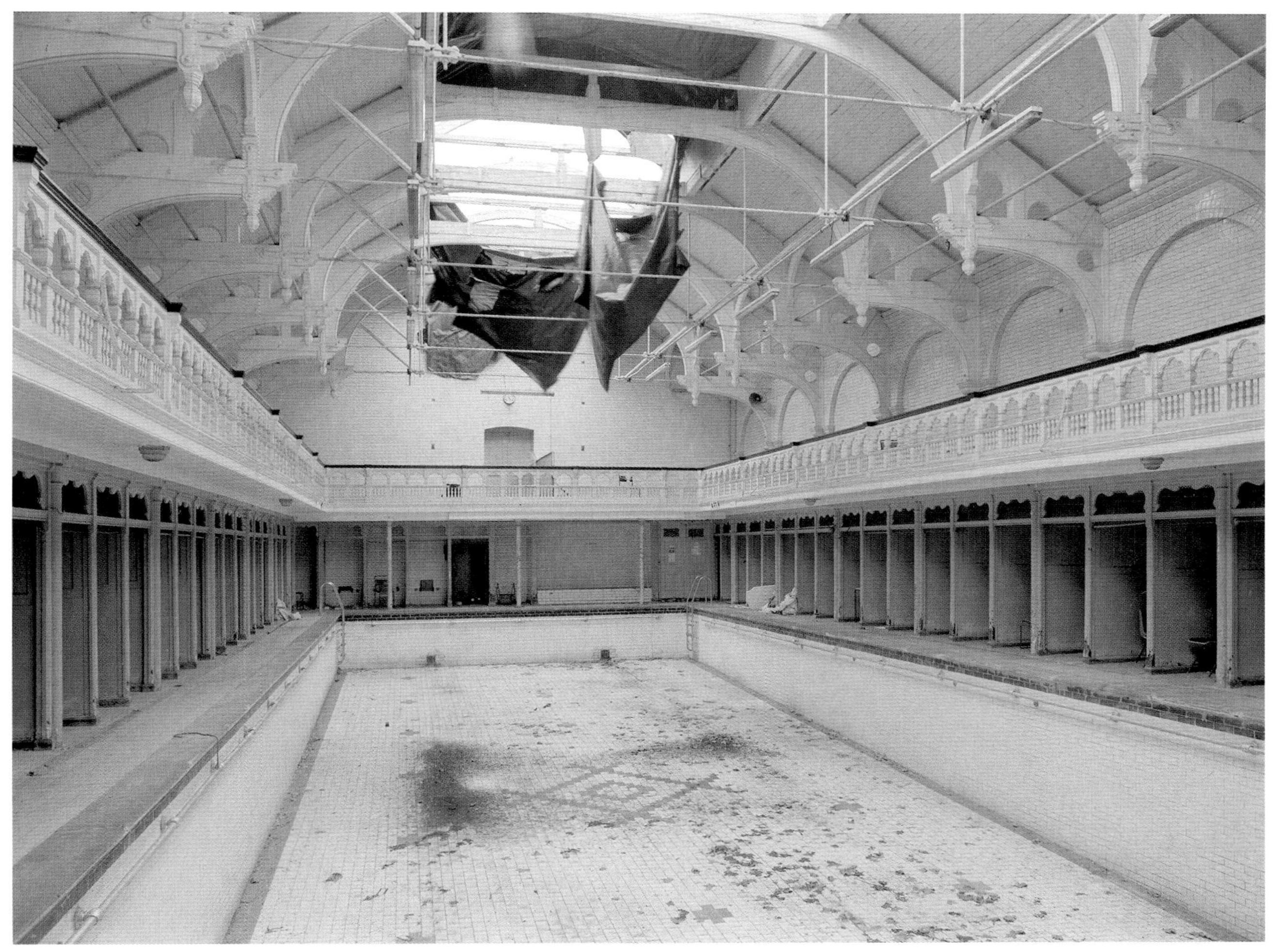

Ladies' Pool at Hackney Public Baths E5, 1986

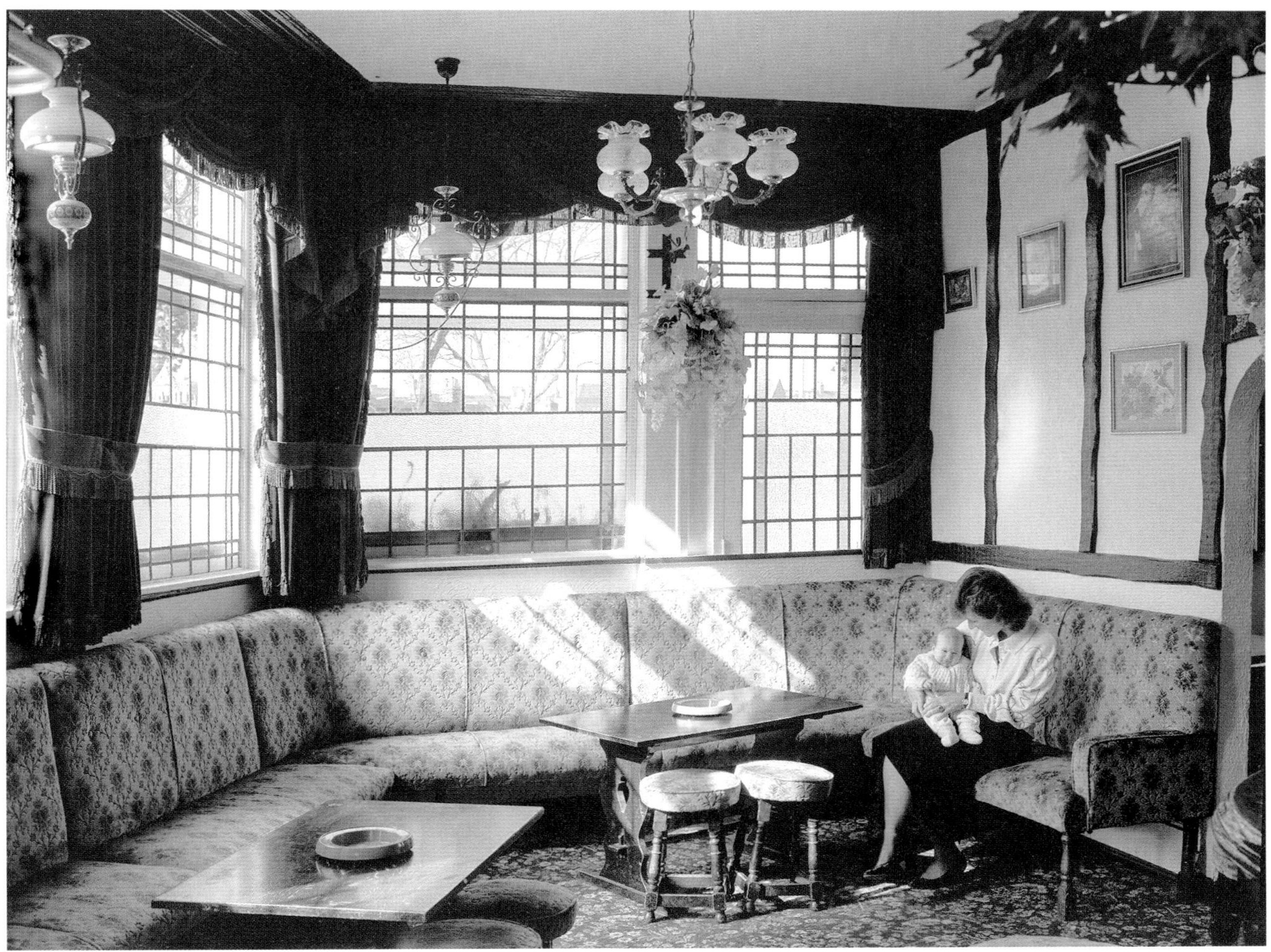

Kenton Arms E9, 1986

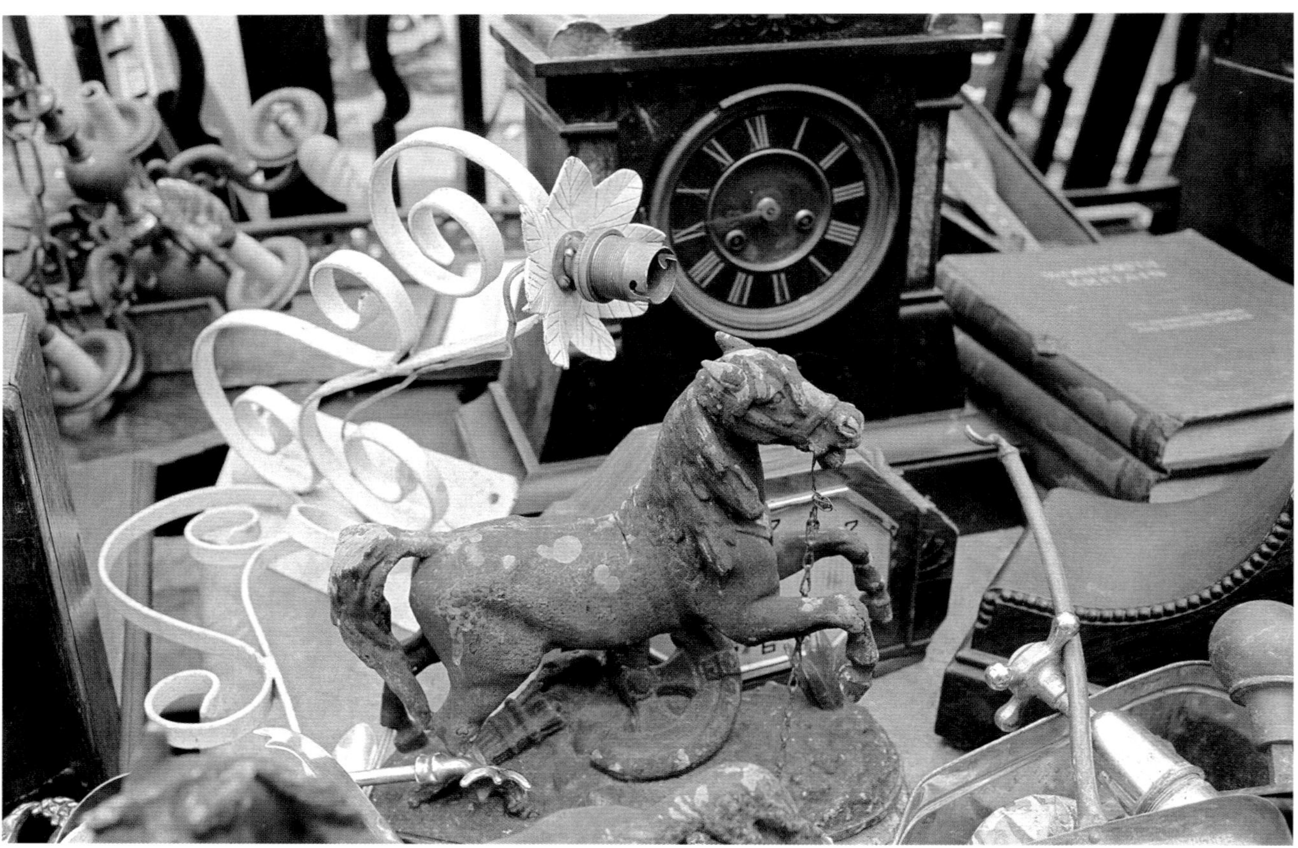

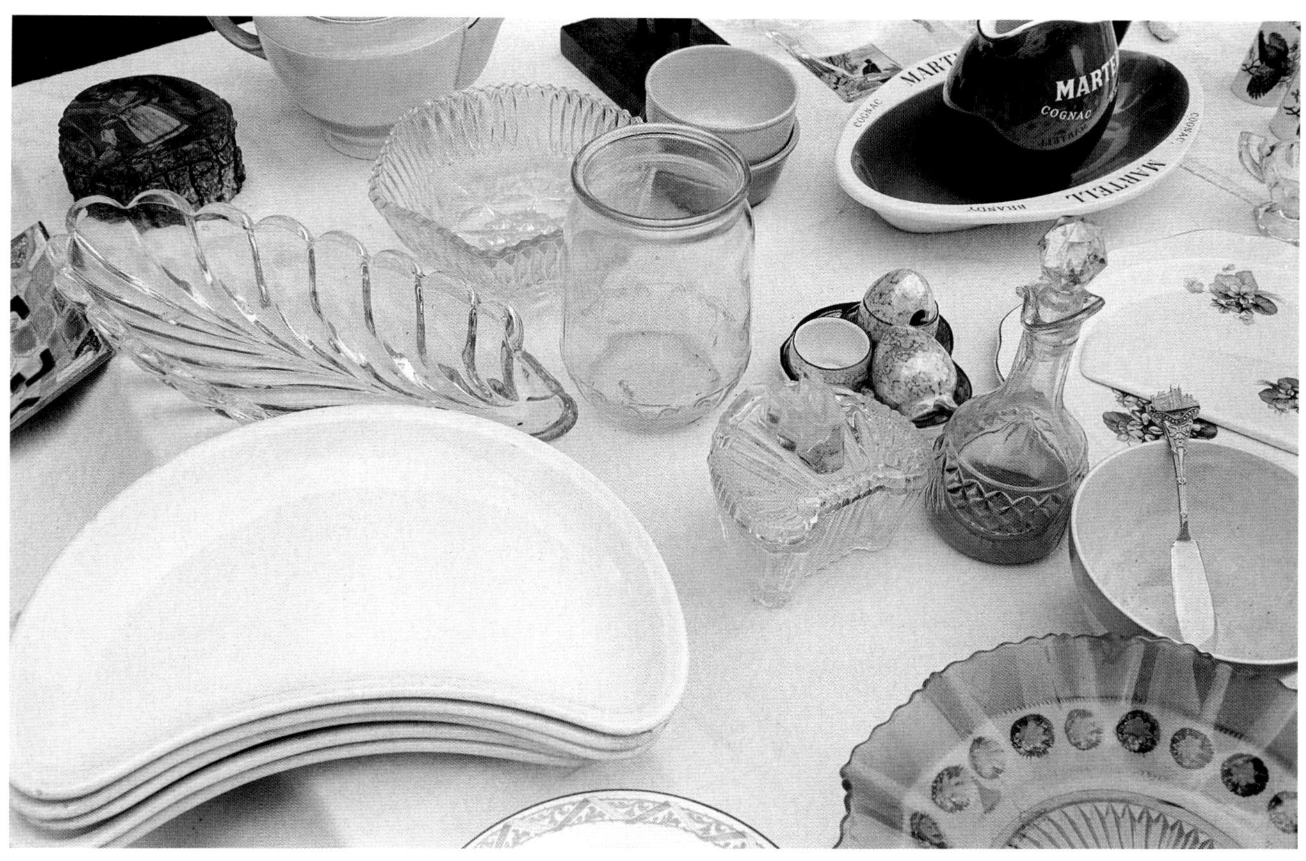

(*both*) Brick Lane E1, 1977

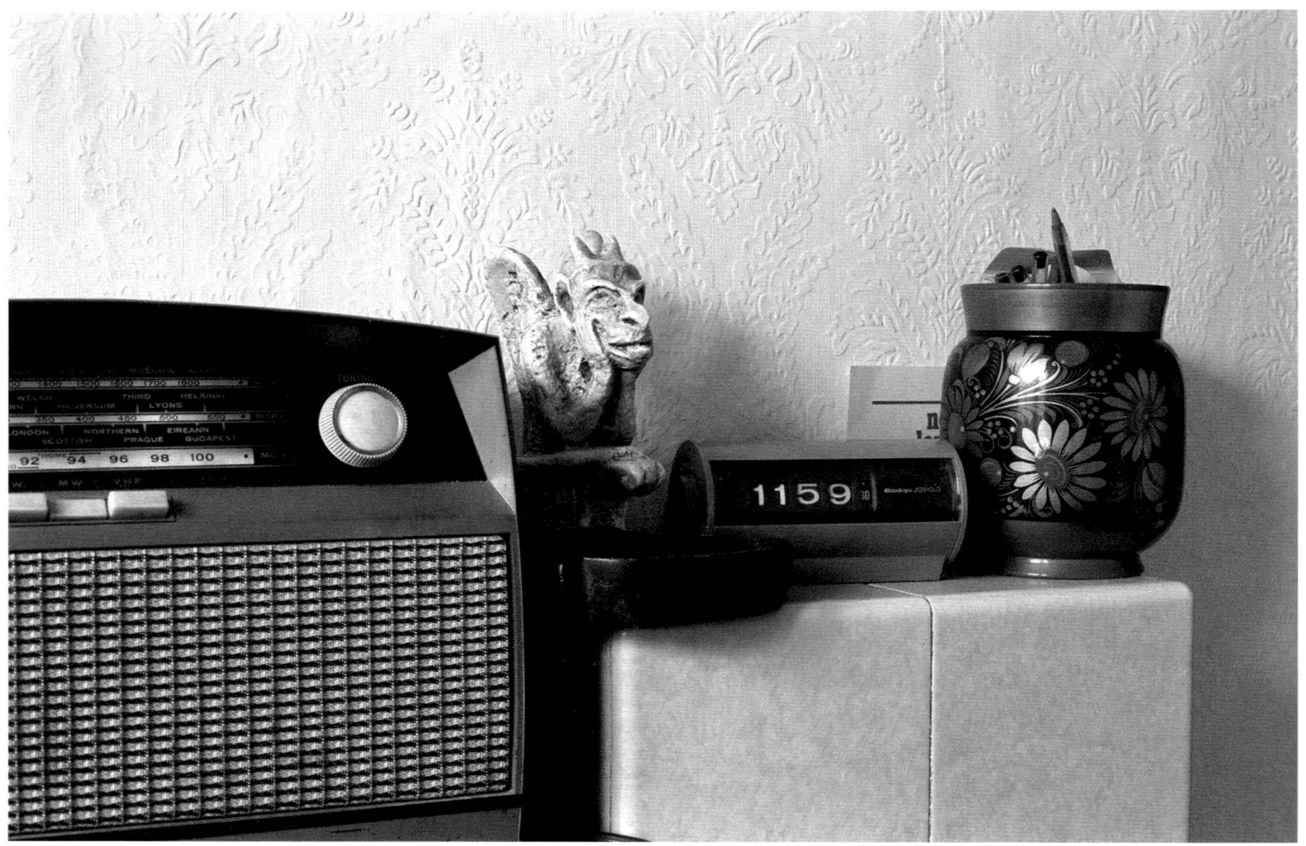

Clapton E5, 1980

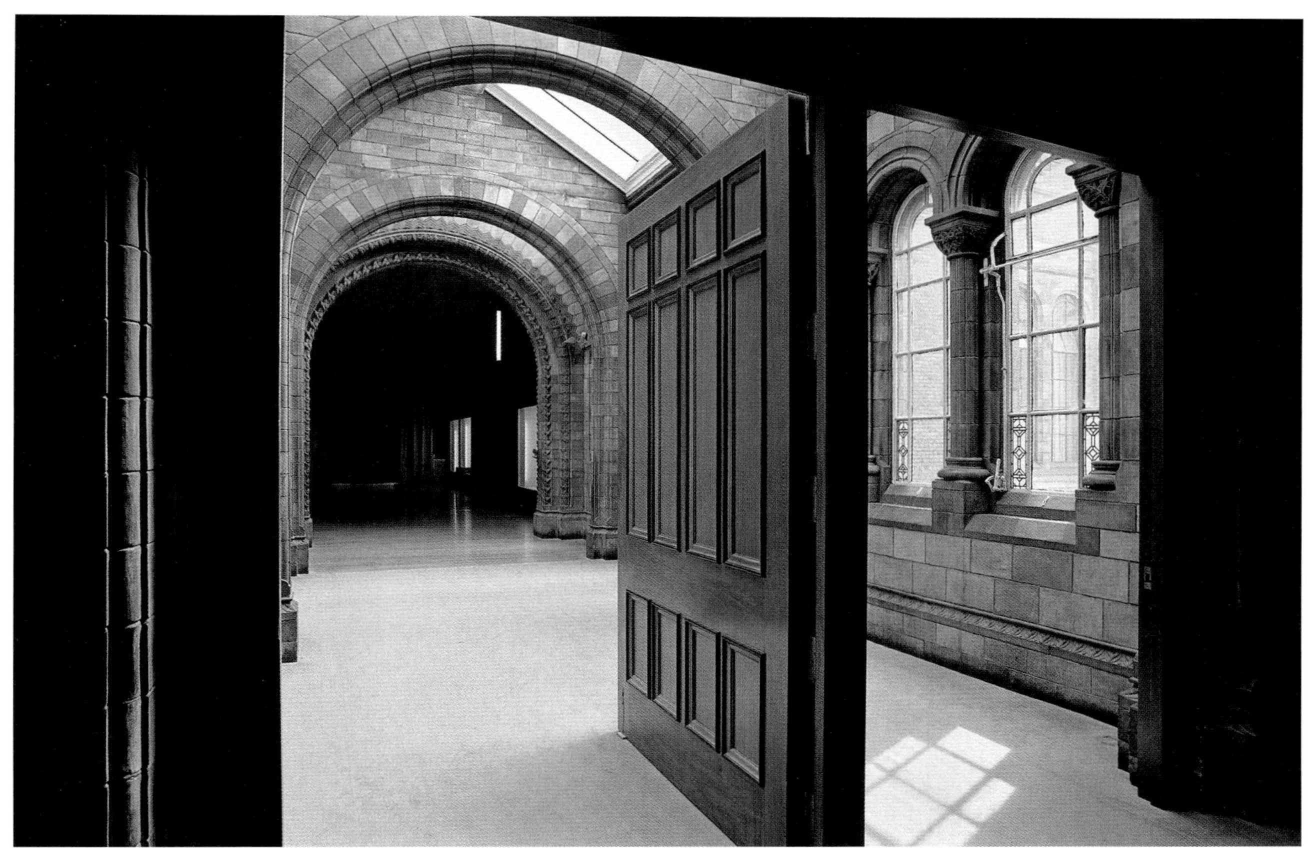

Natural History Museum SW7, 1977

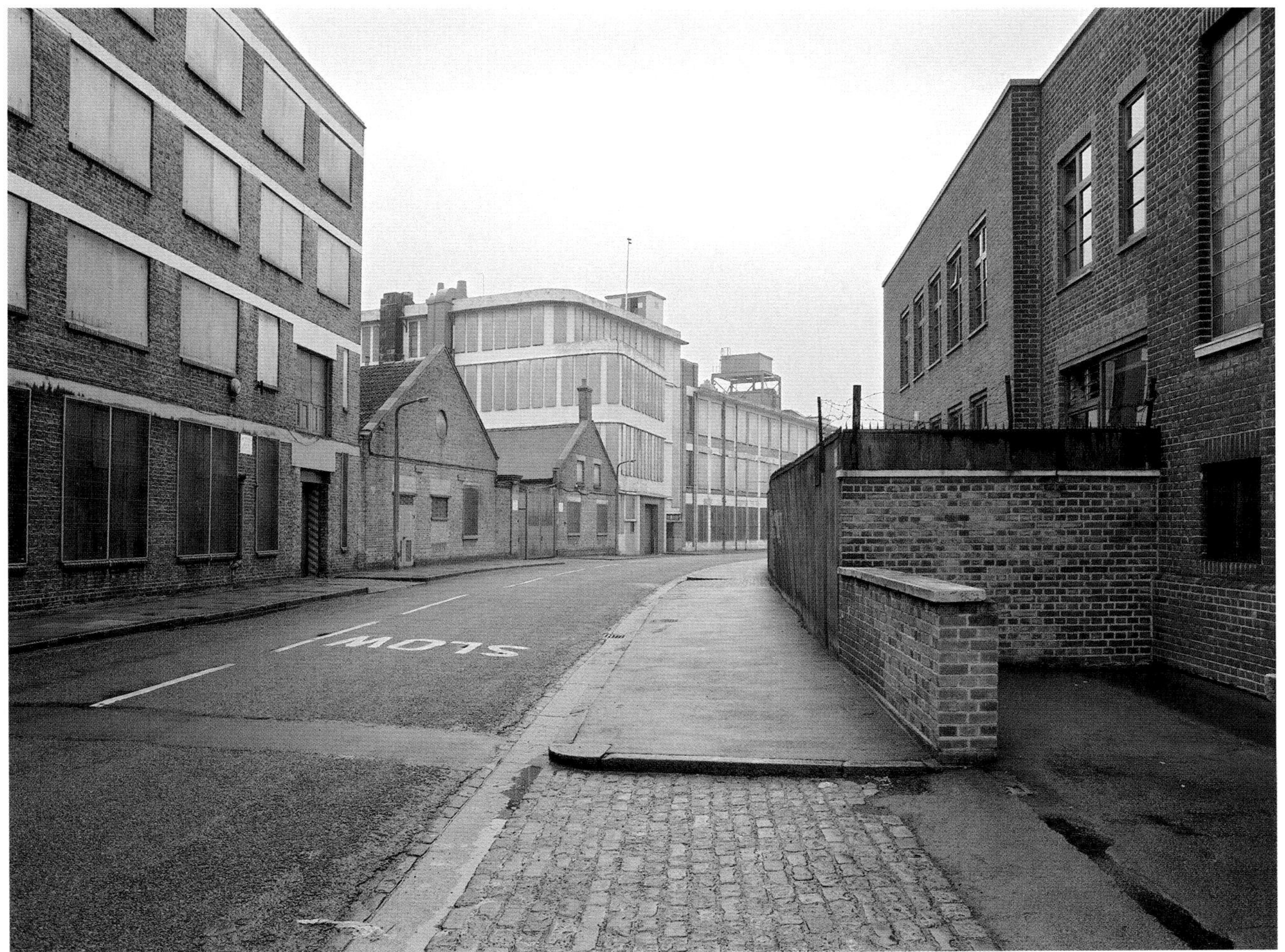

Theydon Road E5, 1987

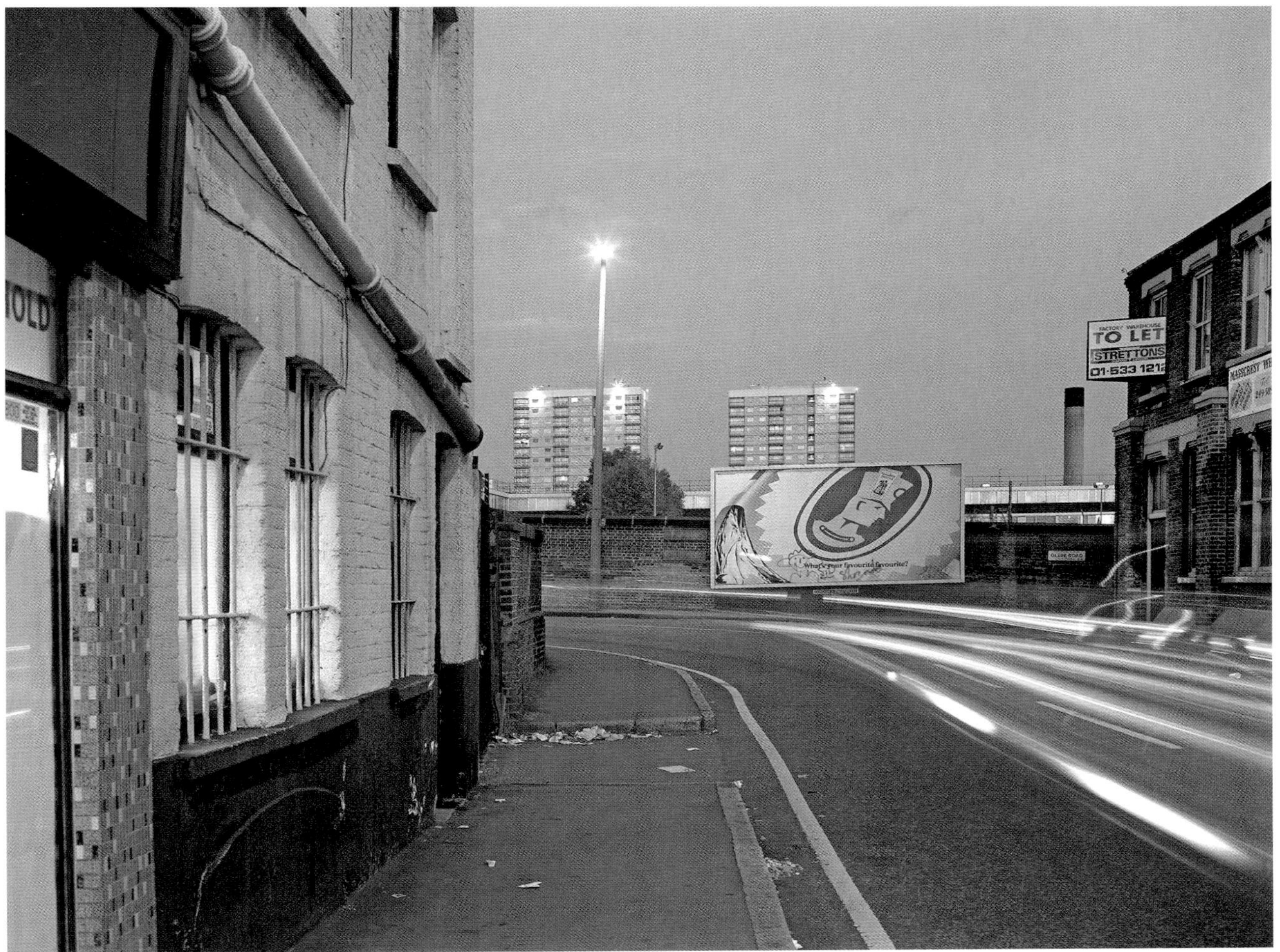

Richmond Road E8, 1985

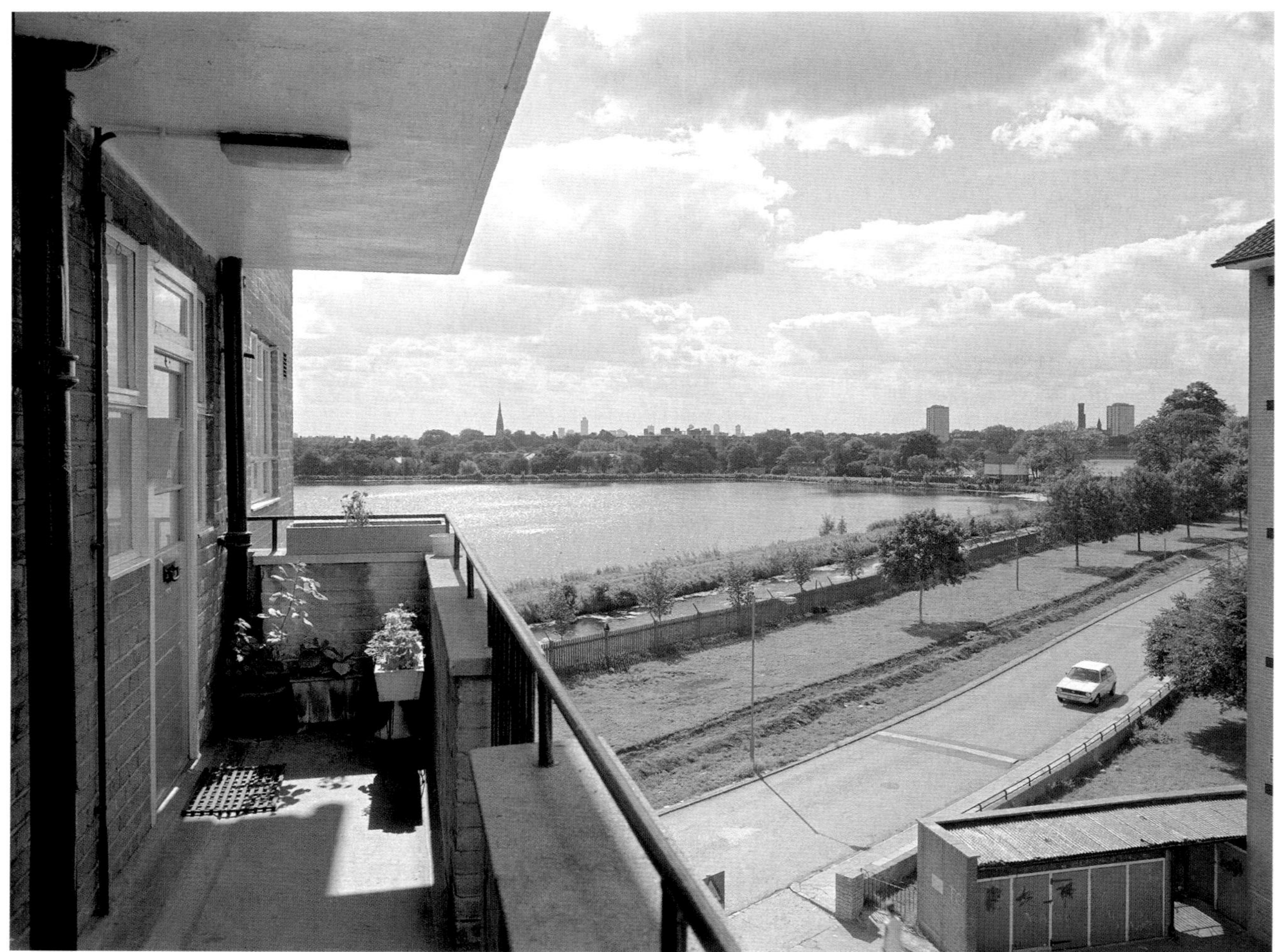

Newnton Close N4, 1987

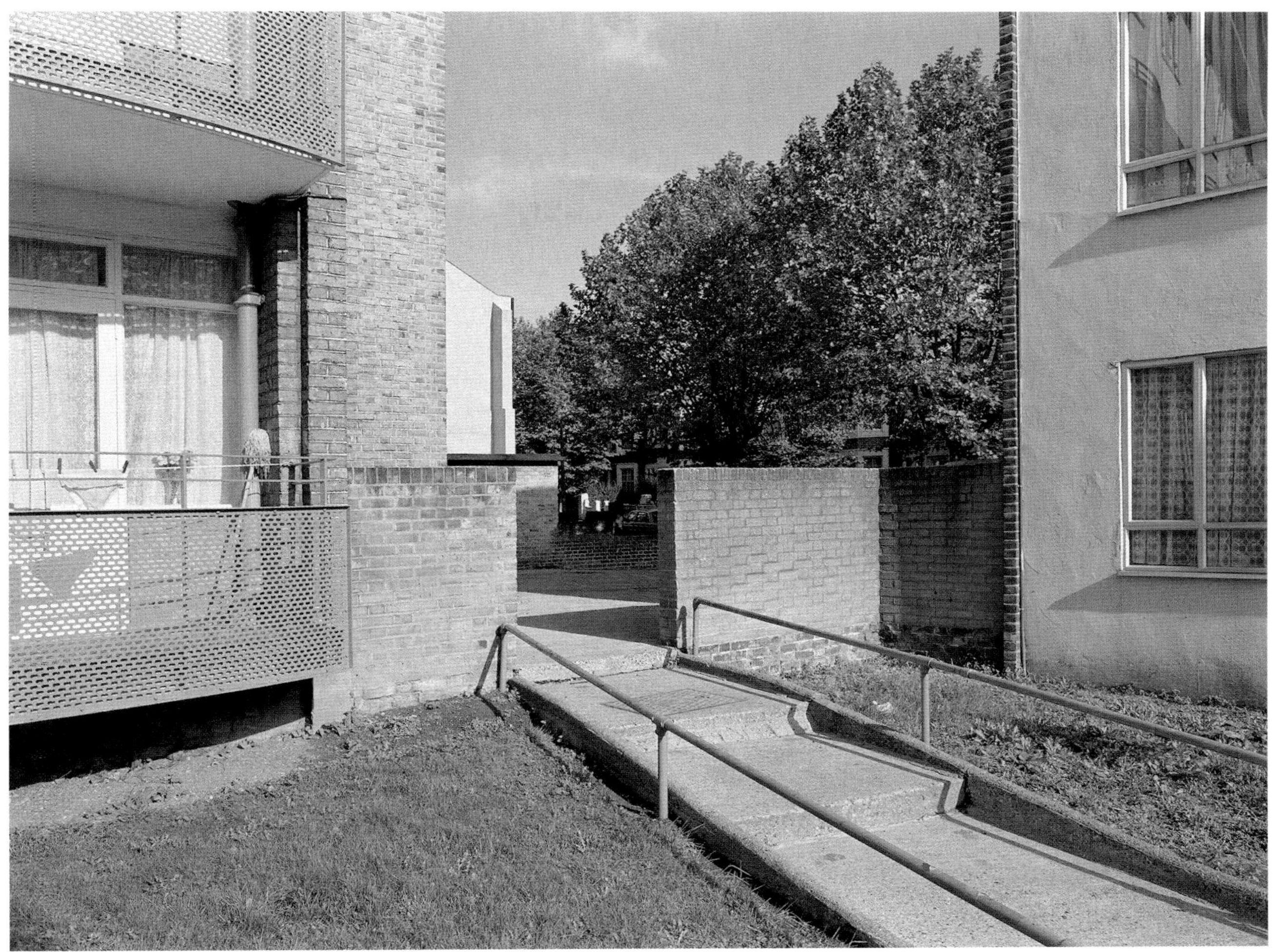

George Downing Estate N16, 1986

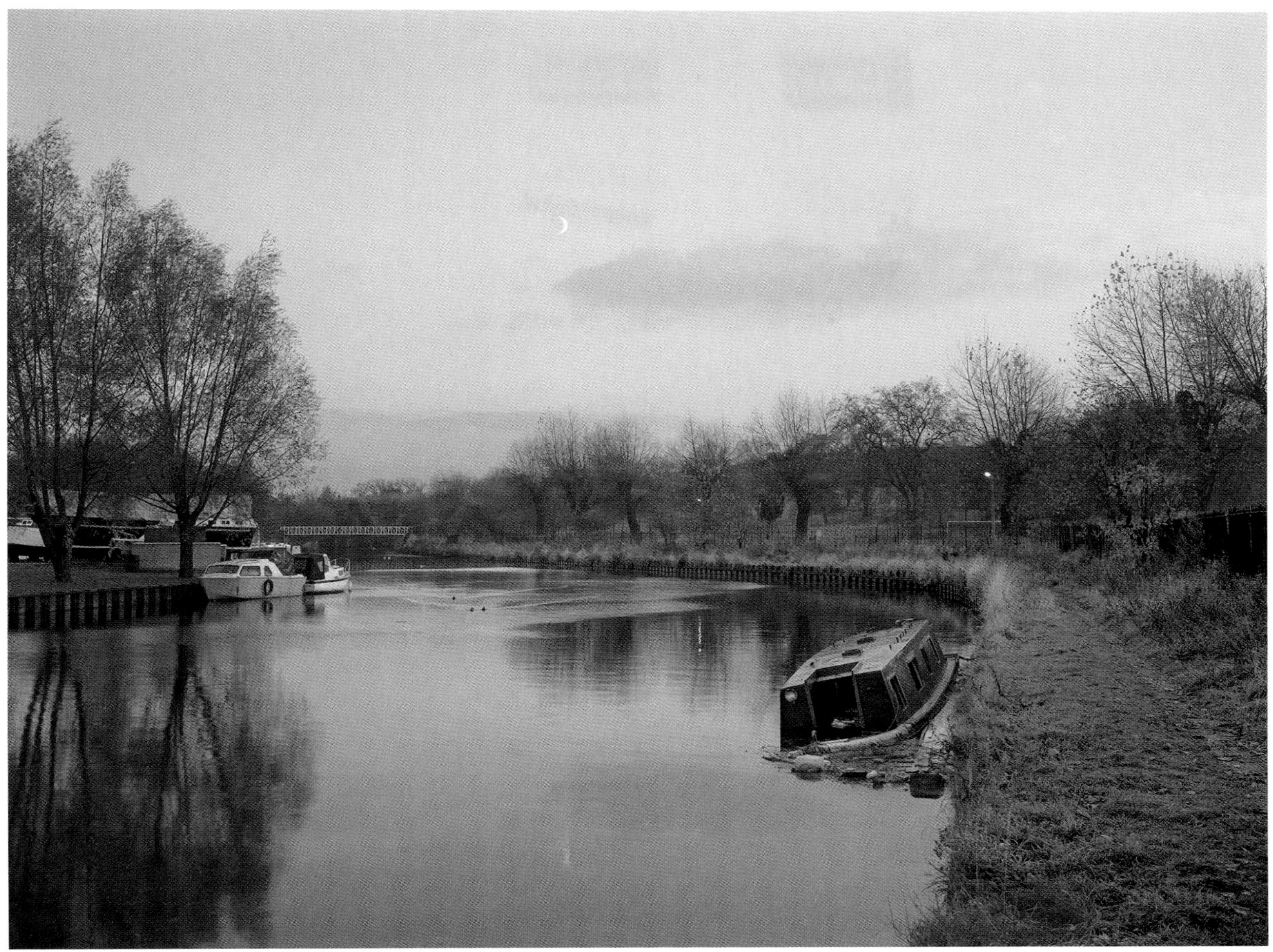

River Lea E5, 1986

London 1977–1987

First edition, published 2021 by Hoxton Mini Press, London

Copyright © Hoxton Mini Press 2021. All rights reserved.
Photographs © Berris Conolly
Introduction © Geoff Nicholson

Design and sequence by Friederike Huber, design support by Daniele Roa,
copy-editing by Florence Filose, production by Anna De Pascale

The right of Berris Conolly to be identified as the creator of this Work has been asserted
under the Copyright, Designs and Patents Act 1988. No part of this publication may
be reproduced, stored in a retrieval system, or transmitted in any form or by any means,
electronic, mechanical, photocopying, recording or otherwise, without the prior
written permission of the copyright owner.

ISBN: 978-1-914314-04-9

A CIP catalogue record for this book is available from the British Library.

Printed and bound by Livonia, Latvia

This book is 100% carbon compensated according to ClimateCalc (climatecalc.eu).
Offset purchased from: Stand for Trees.

For every book you buy from our website, we plant a tree:
www.hoxtonminipress.com

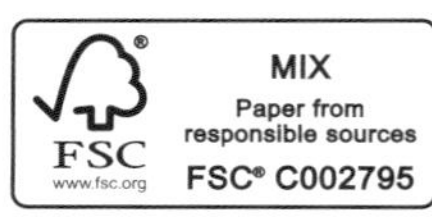